UNHEARD SCREAMS:
The Hidden War on (Wo)men

Prof. Sandra C. Duru

UNHEARD SCREAMS: The Hidden War on (Wo)men by
Prof. Sandra C. Duru

A Comprehensive Handbook on Sexual Harassment, Gender-Based Harassment, Discrimination, Intimidation, Gender Weaponization, Bullying Against (Wo)men, and innocent persons who have no voice and influence, and are being victimized because they have no one to stand for them. No one should ever suffer such, regardless of their gender, beliefs, age, creed, or color!

Published by Mgbeke Media Publishing

Visit the author's website at www.mgbeke.com
Copyright © 2025 by Sandra Duru

All rights reserved. No portion of this book may be reproduced in any form without permission from the author except as permitted by U.S. copyright laws. To ask for permission, contact: info@mgbeke.media

Cover by Empress Creations

ISBN
Paperback: 979-8-9865706-

Printed in the United States of America
First Edition

Disclaimer: As much as this book references some actual events and real-life experiences and is not a body of fiction, the names of some characters herein have been changed to protect the parties' privacy. While some references are direct quotes from the duly named parties, any other similarities to unintended parties are coincidental, and the author assumes no liability for allegations of harm therefrom. Moreover, some of the information herein is not to be taken as an attestation of criminal conduct. Hence, the author assumes no liability for action taken because of the information herein. The author also assures that, as much as many direct references are made to The Bible and Christian faith, this is in no way an attempt to coerce, force it on, or unsettle anyone or any other religion. Inspiration is everywhere around us in nature, and it thrives when there is a spiritual connection that the author profoundly enjoys, hence the frequent references.

Acknowledgment

This book is dedicated to every woman, man, girl, and boy who has ever been harassed, bullied, intimidated, or discriminated against. Your voice matters. Your fight is valid. And your victory is coming.

A special appreciation also goes out to the fearless men and women who have inspired this work, especially those who fought, those who spoke, and those who refused to give up. You are the beacons of light for those without voices or the strength to stand up for themselves, and as sure as each night must always give way to the day at dawn, posterity will surely remember you all, and it will certainly be for good!

Foreword

The world has long prided itself on progress, including technological advancements, legal reforms, and movements advocating for human rights. Yet, despite this progress, one war remains largely unspoken: the relentless battle against sexual harassment, gender-based violence, gender weaponization, discrimination, intimidation, and bullying faced by women, men, girls, and boys worldwide.

People around the world, especially in Africa, continue to face oppression in various forms. In their homes, they are silenced. In schools, they are harassed. In workplaces, they are undermined. In politics, they are threatened. Their screams for justice are often unheard, drowned by cultures of impunity, patriarchy, emotional manipulation, gender weaponization, and corruption.

This book, **"Unheard Screams: The Hidden War on (Wo)men"**, is not just a handbook; it is a weapon, a guide, and a voice for the voiceless. It is designed to empower women, men, girls, and boys, providing them with the knowledge, courage, and strategies needed to recognize, report, and resist harassment, discrimination, and intimidation.

By highlighting real-life cases of women and men who fought back, exposing systemic failures, and providing legal frameworks, this book seeks to educate and inspire. Every human being deserves to live in dignity, free from fear and oppression. It is time to turn silent screams into a collective roar that can no longer be ignored.

This is not just a book. It is a movement. It is a revolution!

About The Author

Prof. Sandra C. Duru is a media scientist, public relations expert, renowned scholar, public administrator, and entrepreneur. A fierce advocate for men's and women's rights, she has fearlessly confronted corruption, harassment, and oppression.

Through her work, she continues to inspire men, women, boys, and girls to stand up, speak out, and fight for justice. She is a remarkable mother of three lovely children and several adopted children worldwide. She continues to be an exemplary motivation, role model, and leader through her publications, daily social media posts, and other projects.

Introduction

Why This Book? For far too long, men and women have been told to endure, to adapt, and to stay silent. When a person speaks out against harassment or injustice, they are often met with ridicule, threats, or even violence. The world expects them to be strong, yet it also demands their submission.

This handbook is written for every woman, man, girl, and boy who has ever felt powerless, every survivor who has been shamed into silence, and every fighter who refuses to back down. It is for the students harassed by their professors, the employees blackmailed by their bosses, the politicians undermined by their counterparts, and the parents silenced within their own homes.

But this book is not just about problems; it is about solutions. It provides a clear, structured, and practical approach to understanding, preventing, and fighting sexual harassment, gender weaponization, and gender-based discrimination. It offers real-life case studies, legal insights, and strategies for self-advocacy.

I must also add that this book is by no means an attack on any gender but a conscious, deliberate, well-needed, and pretty much overdue call for every affected person to rise for themselves and others around them and refuse to continue being weak pawns in the hands of many corrupted beings, no matter what they label themselves. Hence, I have specially coined the word ***"(wo)man"***: a joint word meaning woman and man, to help pass my message across more effortlessly.

And as much as we have chosen to cry out against this discrimination, it would be hypocritical and shameful not to admit that every man out there is not a beast and predator, because I know that they are sadly always the first "suspects" whenever a female cries foul. There are still many honorable, dignified, Godly, and genuinely loving ones among them, and for every one of such out there who still knows and understands that it is a male's divine right and duty to protect every female around him, especially his special female. May the Almighty God continue to bless, strengthen, keep, and enrich you greatly. Amen!

Finally, it is my earnest desire that this signature slogan and the clarion call to action below that I coined become our unique anthem worldwide as we band together to rid ourselves of the scourge and plague of sexual harassment, gender weaponization, intimidation, victimization, bullying, and every work of such vile predators.

Anthem: *"I am a (wo)man! I am strong! I am enough! I am the chance to bring a positive change to the world!"*

Call To Action (Triple R): *"Rise, Resist, Reclaim what belongs to you: your rights, your dignity, and your future!"*

Personal Note from Prof. Sandra C. Duru

I have lived this battle. I have faced harassment, intimidation, and systemic attacks simply because I refused to bow to corruption and oppression. I have been blacklisted, called names, and threatened, but I refused to be silenced. And I am not alone.

Women and men across Africa and the world are fighting battles they never signed up for. Many are bullied out of their careers, silenced in academia, and ridiculed in politics. Others are abused within their homes and trapped in relationships where their voices hold no weight.

But I say this to every woman and man reading this book: You are not alone. You are powerful. And your voice matters!

I wrote **"Unheard Screams: The Hidden War on (Wo)men"** because our silence is their weapon, and it is time to take that weapon away from those who unjustly victimize, assault, harass, and viciously silence us. This book is about knowledge, and knowledge is power. When you know your rights, you become dangerous to oppressors.

Remember this:

"When a corrupt system sees a fearless woman rising, they panic. When that woman knows her rights, they tremble. And when she stands firm, they fall!" – Prof. Sandra C. Duru.

A Call to Action: (Wo)men, Rise!

This is not just a book; it is a battle cry. It is time for women, men, girls, and boys to rise, speak out, and fight back.

To the women and men in workplaces: Demand respect, challenge biases, and report harassment and gender weaponization.

To the young girls and boys in schools: Educate yourselves, reject intimidation, and call out abuse.

To the women and men in politics: Take your space, stand your ground, and never be silenced.

To the men who stand with us: Be allies, challenge toxic masculinity, and advocate for change.

The war on (wo)men is real, but so is our strength. And with knowledge, unity, chastity, integrity, and resilience, we will win.

Now, let's begin.

Table of Contents

1. Acknowledgment
2. Foreword
3. About The Author
4. Introduction
5. Personal Note From Prof. Sandra C. Duru
6. The Silent Struggle: Unveiling the War on (Wo)men
7. Understanding Sexual Harassment & Gender-Based Violence
8. The Legal Framework & Global Commitments
9. Breaking the Silence: Reporting & Seeking Justice
10. Empowerment Through Knowledge: Knowing Your Rights & Fighting Back
11. From Pain to Power: Turning Personal Battles Into Global Change
12. No One Is Immune From Unheard Screams: A Case Study On Senator Natasha vs. Senator Akpabio
13. How Do The Manipulative Fight? Key Traits Of Gender-Based Propaganda, Manipulation, & Weaponization

14. The Role Of The Law: How The Judicial System Affects Cases Like This
15. Food For Deep Thoughts: Is There A Link Between Social Manipulation & National Security?
16. What To Expect When You Stand For Truth: What Should You Do?
17. A Call To Action: Rise, Resist, Reclaim
18. Appendices
19. 50 Inspirational Quotes by Prof. Sandra C. Duru

Chapter 1:

The Silent Struggle: Unveiling the War on (Wo)men

"This is a guide to understanding the fight, a mirror to reflect your strength, and a spark to ignite change. The silent struggle ends when we start shouting, and we're just getting started." – Prof. Sandra C. Duru.

Have you ever felt like your voice got stuck in your throat, or watched someone you love get crushed under the weight of unfair treatment? This chapter is a great starting point for you.

Welcome to the messy, real-world battle I call the "war on (wo)men": a term I've coined to pull women and men together into this fight. It's not just a catchy phrase; it's a recognition that sexual harassment, gender-based discrimination, intimidation, bullying, and the sneaky tactic of gender weaponization don't pick sides based on gender. They hit everyone: women, men, girls, boys, and often leave the innocent feeling like they have no one in their corner.

Let's get real for a second. This war isn't some distant

headline; it's happening in our backyards, offices, schools, and homes. I want to share some real-life examples with you below to illustrate how far and deep this war runs, and also show that there really isn't a safe spot for anyone until we all rally and eradicate it. Many of the names and details in this book are redacted for privacy and security reasons, but this doesn't make their experiences less real or invalid in any way.

Take workplaces, for instance, and let's look at Jane, a nurse in a bustling hospital in Texas. She dealt with a senior doctor who would toss inappropriate comments her way, as if they were part of the job description. However, when she reported it, hoping for support, she got sidelined, passed over for promotions, her shifts cut, and her confidence chipped away. Or consider Mark, a factory worker in the Midwest, who found himself mocked and demoted after refusing to laugh along with crude jokes about female coworkers. Well, it turns out that toxic masculinity doesn't just hurt women; it can chew up men who dare to step out of line, too.

Now, let's shift to schools, where the war starts young. Aisha, a 16-year-old in Nigeria, shared how a teacher made unwanted advances, leaving her feeling trapped and ashamed.

Unheard Screams: The Hidden War On (Wo)men

She confided in a friend, but the fear of retaliation kept her quiet until a brave classmate helped her report it, sparking a school-wide reckoning. Alternatively, Ethan, a 14-year-old boy in a U.S. high school, faced bullying for not fitting the "tough guy" mold, and his peers constantly jeered at and called him weak for showing empathy. These stories show how early the battle begins, and how innocent kids are shaped before they even know how to fight back.

The political landscape is another gory battlefield on its own. Sarah, a councilwoman in Kenya, took on corrupt officials and faced death threats scrawled on notes slipped under her door. She didn't back down, but the toll was heavy, leading to sleepless nights and a guarded home. Then there's James, a male activist in South Africa, who pushed for gender equality and got undermined by peers who saw his stance as "unmanly." This war is everywhere, and it keeps creeping on. Maria, a mother in Morocco, endured an abusive marriage where her voice was drowned out by control and threats. Meanwhile, Tom, a father in the U.S., lost custody of his kids after his ex-partner's false allegations painted him as a monster. These are all but reminders that this fight cuts both ways.

That's not all, though, and we must talk about the other side of the coin, because fairness matters. False allegations can wreck lives just as much as real abuse.

Unheard Screams: The Hidden War On (Wo)men

Take Brian Banks, a high school football star in California. In 2002, a classmate falsely accused him of rape, derailing his dreams. He spent five years in prison before DNA evidence set him free in 2012, and it is a gut-wrenching example of how the system can turn on innocent men. Or look at John Smith, a UK teacher in 2018, who lost his job and reputation over a baseless claim, and was only cleared after a grueling investigation.

These cases hit hard, showing that while the war on (wo)men is real, we can't ignore the damage of unproven accusations. It's a delicate balance that involves supporting victims while seeking the truth.

So, why am I pouring my heart into this book? Because for too long, we've been told to endure, adapt, and stay silent. Society expects us to be strong and tough it out when a boss makes a lewd remark, shrug off intimidation at school, or swallow abuse at home. Still, it also demands our submission. This double standard is exhausting, and it's time we call it out. This war isn't about blaming one gender; it's about exposing the predators and broken systems that thrive on silence, whether they target women, men, or anyone in between.

Taking a little trip down history lane, we'll find out that this struggle is not a new one. In the 19th century, women like Sojourner Truth fought for recognition, her famous

Unheard Screams: The Hidden War On (Wo)men

"Ain't I a Woman?" speech challenging both racism and sexism. Men, too, faced their battles, like early labor activist Eugene Debs, who stood against exploitation and faced ridicule for advocating fairness across genders. Fast forward to the 20th century, and movements like #MeToo in 2017 brought global attention to harassment. Yet, men like Aziz Ansari faced public backlash over misinterpreted encounters, highlighting the need for nuance. These moments show a long, winding fight, with progress often shadowed by missteps.

Culturally, the war takes different shapes. In Africa, where I've seen this firsthand, patriarchal norms can silence women in rural villages, while urban men face pressure to conform to aggressive stereotypes. In Asia, honor codes sometimes trap women in abusive marriages, while boys are shamed for showing vulnerability. In Europe and the Americas, corporate cultures might favor aggressive masculinity, leaving nonconformists, male or female, on the outs. Everywhere, the common thread is power: those with it use it to oppress, and those without it struggle to be heard.

The stakes are high. Harassment isn't just awkward comments; it is lost jobs, ruined educations, and broken families. But here's the hope: we are not powerless! Every story of resistance shows cracks in the system.

Even false allegation cases prove that truth can prevail with persistence. This chapter isn't just a rundown of problems; it's a wake-up call. I want you to see the war for what it is, feel the weight of these stories, and start thinking about how to fight back. Whether you're a student dodging bullies, a worker facing bias, a parent navigating home struggles, or a leader challenging the status quo, your voice can shake things up.

Let's talk solutions, because awareness is only the first step. Education is key because knowing your rights, like workplace anti-harassment policies or school codes of conduct, gives you leverage. Support networks like friends, colleagues, or advocates can also amplify your cry. And action, even small steps like documenting incidents or speaking out, builds momentum. I've seen it work: a group of women in Ghana formed a collective in 2024 to support each other against workplace harassment, and their efforts led to new company policies.

This war on (wo)men is personal to me. I've faced harassment, intimidation, and blocklisting for calling out corruption; stories I'll share later as you read along. But I'm still here, and so are you. This book is my way of saying you're not alone. It's a guide to understanding the fight, a mirror to reflect your strength, and a spark to ignite change. So, grab a coffee, settle in, and let's unpack this together. The silent struggle ends when we start shouting, and we are just getting started.

CHAPTER 2:

Understanding Sexual Harassment & Gender-Based Violence

"The first step toward justice is understanding the injustice." – Prof. Sandra C. Duru.

A wise man once said, "You cannot heal a pain you have never felt," and there is almost no greater truth than this.

The most important aspect of any justice system is not how learned, well-read, astute, or exposed its judges and legal practitioners are. Rather, it is how emotionally intelligent, experienced, empathetic, and humane they are that counts. Hence, delivering genuine justice for a victim of any form of sexual harassment begins with having an in-depth, concise, and holistic knowledge, understanding, and/or experience of what it is all about.

This isn't just a dry topic; it's the heartbeat of the "Hidden War on (Wo)men" that I'm calling out in this book. Whether you're a woman, man, girl, or boy, this stuff affects us all, and it's time we get real about what it looks like, why it happens, and how we can fight back. So, let us break this down together now.

What is Sexual Harassment?

Sexual harassment is any unwelcome sexual advance, request for sexual favors, or other verbal or physical conduct of a sexual nature that creates an intimidating, hostile, or offensive environment. It is that creepy, unwanted behavior like lewd comments, unwanted touching, or pressure for favors. It's not just the obvious stuff; it can be the sly remarks that make you feel small or the jokes that cross a line.

It happens in homes, schools, workplaces, religious institutions, and even online. It can be subtle (unwanted jokes, inappropriate comments) or overt (physical assault, threats, coercion).

Examples of Sexual Harassment:

- A professor demanding sexual favors in exchange for grades.
- A male colleague making inappropriate sexual jokes about a female coworker, or vice versa.
- A political opponent using sexual slurs to discredit a female candidate.
- A husband forcing his wife into sexual acts against her will.
- A boss sending explicit messages to an employee under the pretense of mentorship.
- Cyber harassment: Threats, revenge porn, and unwanted sexual messages on social media.

To further break it down with some real stories, meet Imani, a 19-year-old student in Kenya. She faced a professor who made suggestive comments during tutorials, leaving her dreading class. She didn't know how to report it until a friend pointed her to a school counselor. Then there's James, a warehouse worker in South Africa, who endured crude jokes from coworkers about his masculinity, which escalated to threats when he pushed back. In a home setting, remember Maria from Morocco, who suffered years of emotional abuse from her husband, her pleas ignored by family elders. These aren't just names but snapshots of a war that is personal and pervasive.

What is Gender-Based Violence?

Gender-based violence (GBV) refers to any harmful act directed at an individual based on their gender. While men can also experience gender-based violence, women and girls are disproportionately affected due to societal power imbalances.

This is the broader beast because it inflicts physical, emotional, or psychological harm tied to someone's gender. This could be domestic abuse, workplace intimidation, or even systemic discrimination that keeps people down because of who they are.

Types of Gender-Based Violence:

1. Physical Violence: Domestic abuse, assault, female genital mutilation (FGM).
2. Emotional/Psychological Violence: Gaslighting, public humiliation, intimidation.
3. Sexual Violence: Rape, sexual exploitation, marital rape, trafficking.
4. Economic Violence: Preventing women from accessing financial resources, employment, or education.
5. Political Violence: Threats, harassment, or exclusion of women in politics and leadership roles.

The Cultural and Institutional Roots of Harassment

Why does this keep happening? Power is the root. Harassers and abusers thrive on control, exploiting imbalances, be it gender, age, or status, and systemic failures amplify it.

In many places, weak laws or corrupt enforcement let offenders off easy. Take the 2024 report from Kenya, where only 10% of harassment cases led to convictions due to poor investigation. Cultural silence also plays a role, as society often blames victims, asking "What did you do?" instead of "Who did this?" Hence, emotional manipulation keeps victims quiet.

Sexual harassment and gender-based violence do not exist in isolation. They are deeply rooted in culture, tradition, and systemic inequalities.

- Patriarchy: The belief that men should dominate society and women should submit.
- Religious and Cultural Justifications: Some traditions wrongly justify women's oppression.
- Legal Gaps and Corruption: Weak laws and corrupt systems often protect perpetrators instead of victims.
- Victim Blaming: Society often shames survivors instead of holding perpetrators accountable.

Why Do Women Stay Silent?

Many women and girls do not report harassment because of:

- Fear of Retaliation: Losing their jobs, failing exams, or facing social ostracization.
- Lack of Trust in the System: Corrupt institutions often dismiss or ignore cases.
- Shame and Stigma: Society often blames victims instead of perpetrators.
- Financial Dependence: Many women endure abuse because they have nowhere else to go.

Unheard Screams: The Hidden War On (Wo)men

Recognizing the Signs

So, how do we spot this? Sexual harassment can be overt, like catcalls, groping, or subtle, persistent "jokes" or stares. Gender-based violence might be a slap, a threat, or constant belittling. Red flags include feeling unsafe, pressured, or dismissed. Imani noticed her professor lingering too long; James felt the shift when coworkers turned hostile. Learning these signs is step one, and you must go through it because knowledge is your shield.

Taking The First Step & Breaking the Silence

The only way to end this war is for men and women to speak up and for every gender to be held accountable. Silence protects oppressors; courage liberates victims.

You're not powerless. Education is key, so you must know your rights, like Nigeria's 2015 Violence Against Persons Act. Support helps, and a supportive teacher or friend can be a much-needed lifeline. Also, the most important action starts small, like documenting incidents, which can build a case.

This chapter isn't just an eye-opener; it's a toolkit. Whether you're a student, worker, or parent, understanding this war is how we begin to win. So, let's keep going, because your voice matters!

CHAPTER 3:

The Legal Framework & Global Commitments

"Laws mean nothing if they are not enforced. Rights mean nothing if we do not know them." – Prof. Sandra C. Duru.

Women and men across the world suffer harassment, discrimination, and violence, not because laws do not exist, but because these laws are often ignored, manipulated, or outright unenforced. So, let's dive into the backbone of this fight, which is the legal framework and global commitments that can shield men from the silent war of sexual harassment, gender-based violence, and discrimination.

This chapter explores the legal protections available, both globally and within Africa, to empower women with the knowledge needed to fight back. It isn't just about dry laws; it's about how these tools can empower guys like you who've been targeted, giving you the ammo to stand tall. Whether you're a worker, student, or father, the law is on your side, or at least, it should be.

Remember that even though Esau had despised his birthright and sold it cheaply to his brother Jacob, he was not left to rot in damnation forever by the Almighty, as this scripture in Genesis 24:7 clearly shows:

Unheard Screams: The Hidden War On (Wo)men

"By your sword you shall live, and you shall serve your brother; but when you grow restless you shall break his yoke from your neck."

Therefore, no matter what situations or circumstances have hitherto enslaved you in any entrapments of such discrimination, violence, and harassment, please know today that you have the right and power to break free and live a better life from the day you decide you've had enough. That day starts now, and we'll share some of the liberating knowledge you need in this chapter.

The Legal Landscape: What Is Out There?

Firstly, what is a legal framework? It is the set of laws, policies, and court rulings designed to protect people from abuse and hold offenders accountable. For men, this can mean laws against harassment, violence, or unfair treatment based on gender. Globally, commitments like the United Nations' Convention on the Elimination of All Forms of Discrimination Against Women (CEDAW) and the Sustainable Development Goals (SDGs) push for equality, but they often overlook male victims. That is where national laws come in, and they vary wildly.

Take Nigeria, for instance. The 2015 Violence Against Persons (Prohibition) Act (VAPP) covers harassment and abuse, but enforcement is spotty, and men are rarely seen as victims. Meet Ade, a 34-year-old teacher in Lagos, who faced false accusations of misconduct from a female colleague in 2023. He turned to VAPP, but the process dragged on for months, leaving him jobless until a local NGO stepped in with legal aid. Or consider Musa, a factory worker in Kano, who endured workplace bullying, crude jokes, and threats, yet found no clear legal recourse until a labor union pushed his case under the Labour Act.

In the U.S., Title VII of the Civil Rights Act of 1964 bans workplace discrimination, including gender-based harassment. This helped someone like Jamal, a 28-year-old engineer in Chicago, who was mocked for taking paternity leave in 2024. He filed a complaint, and with help from the Equal Employment Opportunity Commission (EEOC), he won a settlement.

However, not every man is so lucky because legal aid is scarce, and cases can stall. In the UK, the Equality Act 2010 offers protection, yet David, a 40-year-old nurse in Manchester, faced intimidation from coworkers and struggled to prove it, highlighting gaps in enforcement.

Global Commitments: Are They Enough?

Globally, treaties aim to level the playing field. The SDGs, especially Goal 5 on gender equality, call for ending all forms of violence, but the focus often tilts toward women. Men like Kwame, a 22-year-old student in Ghana, fall through the cracks. Harassed by a peer, he found no support under local SDG-aligned programs.

The Beijing Declaration from 1995, signed by 189 countries, pushes for gender equity, but its implementation rarely addresses male victimization. For instance, Bakari, a 35-year-old farmer in rural Kenya, who faced domestic violence from his wife, had his plea dismissed by community leaders citing cultural norms over global pledges.

Thankfully, progress is brewing, though, as the 2023 UN Resolution on Gender-Based Violence and Harassment included language on male victims. International bodies like the International Labour Organization (ILO) also updated its 2019 Violence and Harassment Convention (No. 190) to cover all genders, offering hope for men.

The UN Charter on Gender Discrimination and Sexual Harassment

The United Nations (UN) has long recognized that sexual harassment and gender-based violence are violations of human rights. It is also one of several international agreements that outline global commitments to gender equality and the protection of women.

Key International Agreements:

1. The Universal Declaration of Human Rights (1948)
- Affirms the equal rights of all human beings, regardless of gender.

2. The Convention on the Elimination of All Forms of Discrimination Against Women (CEDAW) (1979)
- Often referred to as the "Bill of Rights for Women."
- Requires countries to adopt policies and laws that protect women from discrimination and violence.

3. The Beijing Declaration and Platform for Action (1995)
- Identifies violence against women as a major obstacle to gender equality.
- Calls for stronger laws, support systems, and societal change.

4. The International Labour Organization (ILO) Convention on Violence and Harassment (2019)
- Recognizes sexual harassment in the workplace as a serious issue and urges governments to enforce strict penalties.

What Does This Mean for Women?

These global commitments mean that no woman should feel powerless. Governments worldwide are legally obligated to prevent, investigate, and punish sexual harassment and gender-based violence. If they fail, women and advocacy groups have the right to demand accountability.

African Laws and Policies Protecting Women

Africa has some of the strongest women's rights policies on paper, but enforcement remains weak. Many women suffer because corruption, cultural bias, and weak judicial systems protect perpetrators rather than victims.

Nigeria

- The Violence Against Persons (Prohibition) Act (VAPP) 2015:
- Criminalizes sexual harassment, domestic violence, and harmful practices against women.
- Provides compensation and legal protection for victims.
- The Sexual Harassment Prohibition Bill (2020):
- Targets harassment in educational institutions, protecting female students from exploitation.

South Africa

- The Sexual Offenses Act (2007):

- Clearly defines and punishes various forms of sexual harassment and assault.
- Employment Equity Act (1998):
- Prohibits sexual harassment in the workplace.

Kenya

- The Sexual Offenses Act (2006):
- Provides strict penalties for rape, defilement, and sexual harassment.
- Protection Against Domestic Violence Act (2015):
- Recognizes emotional and psychological abuse as a form of violence.

Ghana

- Domestic Violence Act (2007):
- Criminalizes all forms of gender-based violence.
- Labour Act (2003):
- Includes provisions against sexual harassment at work.

Namibia

- Combating of Rape Act 8 of 2000
- The Combating of Domestic Violence Act
- Married Persons Equality Act

The Gaps and Failures

Despite these laws, women rarely get justice. Many cases go unreported due to:

- Fear of retaliation.
- Corrupt law enforcement.
- Cultural and religious biases.

This is why women must not only know their rights but also demand their enforcement.

Legal Rights of Women: How to Seek Justice

Knowing the law is one thing; using it to fight back is another. Here's how women can navigate the legal system to seek justice when faced with harassment or discrimination.

Steps to Take When Harassed:

1. Document Everything:
- Keep records of messages, emails, incidents, and witness accounts.
- Screenshots and voice recordings can serve as evidence.

2. Report to the Right Authority:
- Workplace: Human Resources (HR) or a labor rights organization.
- School: University administration, student affairs, or legal bodies.
- Public Spaces: Police, NGOs, or legal aid services.

3. Seek Legal Advice:
- Many organizations offer free legal support for women facing harassment.
- In Nigeria, groups like WARDC (Women Advocates Research and Documentation Centre) can help.

4. Take the Case to Court:
- If internal reporting fails, victims have the right to seek justice.
- Legal action can lead to compensation, criminal penalties, or policy changes.

5. Use Social Media and Public Pressure:
- In cases where legal justice seems impossible, public exposure can force action.
- Many cases gain momentum when activists and the media get involved.

What Happens After Reporting?

- A formal investigation should be initiated immediately.
- The accused has the right to respond but cannot retaliate.
- If guilty, consequences may include job termination, fines, imprisonment, or policy reforms.

Cultural Challenges and Legal Gaps

Culture can make or break these laws. In Africa,

patriarchal systems often paint men as aggressors, not victims. For instance, Ibrahim, a 27-year-old shopkeeper in Uganda, was ridiculed by elders when he reported harassment by a female customer, and his case was ignored under local customs.

In Asia, honor codes silence men too, like Ravi, a 33-year-old clerk in India, who endured workplace taunts but feared shaming his family by seeking help. In the West, toxic masculinity adds pressure, as seen in the case of Mark, a 38-year-old teacher in Australia, who was demoted for reporting gender-based bullying, and his complaint was dismissed as weakness.

Historically, laws have evolved slowly. The 19th-century British Offences Against the Person Act laid the groundwork, but men were rarely protected. By the 20th century, movements like the men's rights push in the 1970s in the U.S. challenged this, yet progress lags. In 2024, a European Union directive expanded protections, hence proving that global pressure can shift things.

Can We Make It Work for Men, Too?

How do we use this framework to protect our men, too? We can start with awareness; know your rights. In Nigeria, VAPP requires employers to have anti-harassment policies, so you must know and demand this. Documentation is also key, so always keep a log of incidents to strengthen your case. Legal aid can also bridge gaps, while more countries are pressured to enforce treaties globally.

What are the challenges this move faces?

- Enforcement lags as only 15% of VAPP cases in Nigeria reached court in 2023, per local reports.
- Bias also persists because judges often doubt male victims.
- Resources are thin, and many men cannot afford lawyers.

Notwithstanding, change is possible, as community support and international pressure, like the EU directive, can tip the scales.

Consequences of Sexual Harassment and Gender-Based Violence

Women are not the only victims of harassment; society as a whole suffers. When (wo)men are silenced:

- Workplaces lose talent.
- Children drop out of school.
- Women in politics are pushed out.
- Families suffer emotional and financial trauma.

The Economic Cost:

- Studies show that companies lose billions due to workplace harassment claims and toxic environments.
- Nations lose skilled professionals when women are bullied out of leadership roles.

The Psychological Cost:

- Women who experience harassment often suffer from depression, PTSD, and anxiety.
- Many survivors lose trust in institutions, leading to social withdrawal.

Fighting Back: (Wo)men Who Challenged the System and Won!

Never let anyone tell or convince you to be silent about the abuse and humiliation you've suffered, or may still be enduring, because "the system is rigged against you as a female in Nigeria and Africa" and "nobody will believe or stand up for you."

That is a blatant and diabolical lie, and there are a few case samples here to prove this to you irrefutably. There are still countless honorable, Godly, and upright men in our society who understand their divine mandate over women, and such will always rally around any female they see being unjustly treated, segregated, harassed, and victimized.

Sadly, too, some women also make unsubstantiated and false allegations against men, even in high places, and this is the evil of gender weaponization we must all rally to ensure that this scourge comes to an end in our generation, as clearly witnessed in these case samples below.

1. **Former NDDC Official, Joy Nunieh vs. Senator Godswill Akpabio**

- The former Acting Managing Director of the Niger Delta Development Commission (NDDC) publicly accused the current Nigerian Senate President, Godswill Akpabio, of alleged sexual harassment while he was the Minister for Niger Delta Affairs in 2020. Her claims were never proven, and Senator Akpabio firmly denied the allegations.

- She refused to back down and also claimed she was threatened, but this was also unsubstantiated. She was later relieved of her role due to alleged insubordination.

- Outcome: The exposure of systemic corruption, insubordination, and possible harassment in Nigerian governance.

2. **Prof. Sandra C. Duru vs. Dr. Ndanusa Akanya & Others**

Unheard Screams: The Hidden War On (Wo)men

- As Principal Consultant to the Nigeria Police Service Commission (PSC) and the Standards Organization of Nigeria (SON), Prof. Sandra faced harassment, bullying, and blacklisting.

- She fought back through legal means and public exposure.

- Outcome: Several powerful men were removed from office, though corruption still fought back.

3. Benjamin Mendy vs. 6 False Accusers!

- On July 14, 2023, former Manchester City footballer and French International, Benjamin Mendy, was declared not guilty of all allegations made against him by six different women who had all claimed to have been assaulted by the footballer at different parties between October 2018 and August 2021. Recall that in October 2020, Mendy was accused of raping a 24-year-old woman and attempting to rape another at his Cheshire home in Manchester, England.

- Outcome: After three grueling years of different trials, it was substantially proved that those allegations were all false, and the footballer was cleared of all charges. Manchester City had put him on unpaid leave after he was charged again in September 2021, and he reportedly wept as a jury acquitted him at his retrial at Chester Crown Court. Those allegations literally wrecked his football career and cost him years of his life.

4. Johnny Depp vs. Amber Heard

- Famous Hollywood ex-couple, Johnny Depp and Amber Heard, made headlines in 2022 when the actor sued his ex-wife for defamation after she indirectly alleged domestic violence and abuse against him in an opinion article she wrote for the Washington Post in 2018, and damaged his career.

- Both parties alleged abuse and domestic violence against each other during the highly publicized case, and Amber also sued him, claiming his lawyer had also made defamatory remarks about her abuse claims.

- Outcome: After a lengthy trial that lasted from April 11 to June 1, 2022, in Fairfax County, Virginia, where both parties presented evidence to back their claims, the jury found Amber guilty of defamation and awarded Johnny $10 million in compensatory damages and $5 million in punitive damages. However, due to state law, the punitive damages were reportedly later reduced to $350,000. Amber was also awarded $2 million in compensatory damages for her countersuit.

5. Neymar Junior vs. Najila Trindade

Unheard Screams: The Hidden War On (Wo)men

- In June 2019, Brazilian model Najila Trindade accused Brazilian International and former Barcelona and Paris Saint-Germain superstar, Neymar Jr., of raping her in a hotel in Paris, France, in May 2019, after they had both met there consensually.

- Neymar vehemently denied the allegations and posted a private 7-minute video on his Instagram to prove that they had communicated and mutually agreed to "meet and greet" at the hotel; the video included intimate pictures Najila had sent to him.

- Outcome: The case was eventually dismissed after a trial that lasted for about 3 months, as prosecutors agreed that Najila's claims were unsubstantiated because she had presented no conclusive evidence of rape against him.

6. Dani Alves vs. Undisclosed Female Accuser

- December 31, 2022: An undisclosed woman accuses Dani Alves of sexual assault in a Barcelona nightclub.

- January 2023: Alves is arrested and held in pre-trial detention.

- February 22, 2024: After a three-day trial, Alves is found guilty and sentenced to 4.5 years in prison.

- March 2024: He posts €1 million bail, is released, and surrenders his passports while awaiting appeal.

- March 28, 2025: A Catalan appeals court unanimously overturns the conviction, citing "gaps, inaccuracies, inconsistencies, and contradictions" in the evidence and testimony, reaffirming the presumption of innocence.

- April 2025: Both the accuser and state prosecutors appeal the acquittal to Spain's Supreme Court, leaving his legal status still hanging.

- Outcome: Despite his acquittal, Dani Alves has already suffered irreparable damage, months in prison, the loss of his career, his family, his reputation, and millions in financial losses, all because of an accusation that collapsed under legal scrutiny. Yet the woman who falsely accused him faces no accountability.

Conclusion: The Law is a Weapon. Use It!

Laws exist to protect men and women, but they only work when we know them and demand their enforcement.

"A woman who knows the law is a woman who cannot be silenced." – Prof. Sandra C. Duru.

Unheard Screams: The Hidden War On (Wo)men

The next chapter will focus on how to report harassment and seek justice effectively, including step-by-step guides and resources.

The fight continues.

CHAPTER 4:

Breaking The Silence: Reporting & Seeking Justice

"Silence is the enemy of justice. Every woman who speaks up weakens the chains of oppression." – Prof. Sandra C. Duru.

Sexual harassment, bullying, discrimination, gender weaponization, and intimidation thrive in silence. Many women and girls suffer in fear, unsure of where to turn or how to fight back. Too many victims have been crushed by sexual harassment, gender-based violence, and discrimination, and their voices have been stolen by shame or fear. But not anymore.

This chapter provides a step-by-step guide on reporting harassment, seeking justice, and protecting oneself from retaliation. This is your playbook for standing up, speaking out, and fighting back. Whether you're a worker or student, you've got the power to reclaim your dignity. So, let's roll up our sleeves and get into it!

The Culture of Silence: Why Women Don't Report

Silence is the enemy's weapon, and for too long, (wo)men have been told to tough it out.

Unheard Screams: The Hidden War On (Wo)men

Whether it's a coworker's lewd joke, a boss's threat, or abuse at home, keeping quiet lets the problem fester. Therefore, reporting isn't just about calling out the bad guys but about taking back control.

Despite laws and policies against sexual harassment, many cases never see the light of day. Women often hesitate to report for several reasons:

• Fear of retaliation: Many perpetrators hold powerful positions and can make life unbearable for victims.
• Shame and stigma: Society often blames women for the harassment they suffer.
• Lack of trust in the system: Women doubt the effectiveness of reporting because many cases are dismissed or ignored.
• Financial dependence: Some women endure harassment at work because they fear losing their jobs.
• Cultural and religious barriers: In some African societies, women are told to "endure" abuse rather than fight back.

But silence only protects the abuser, not the victim. Breaking the silence is the first step toward justice and change.

How to Report Sexual Harassment and Gender-Based Violence

So, how do you start? First, recognize the abuse. Is it unwanted advances, threats, or belittling?

If you experience harassment, discrimination, or bullying, document it and report it immediately. Here's a guide on how to take action:

Step 1: Document the Incident

- Write down details: What happened? When and where did it happen? Who was involved?
- Save evidence: Emails, text messages, social media interactions, and photos can serve as proof.
- Identify witnesses: If anyone was present, their testimonies can support your case.

Step 2: Report to the Appropriate Authority

Where you report depends on where the harassment happened, so please take note of these key directions:

Workplace Harassment

- Report to Human Resources (HR): Every organization should have a reporting process.
- Escalate to management if HR fails to act.
- Seek legal advice from labor unions or women's rights groups.

Harassment in Schools and Universities

- Report to the school administration, student affairs office, or anti-harassment committee.

- Some institutions have hotlines for anonymous reporting.
- If the school refuses to act, escalate the case to an external organization.

Public Harassment or Assault

- Report to the police: Insist on getting a case number and request updates on the investigation.
- Approach human rights organizations if the police fail to act.

Political or Governmental Harassment

- Expose the case to anti-corruption agencies, media outlets, and advocacy groups.
- Use public pressure: Many cases gain attention when brought to social media.

Overcoming Fear: Protecting Yourself from Retaliation

Many women fear retaliation when they report harassment, especially when the perpetrator is a boss, professor, or politician. Here's how to protect yourself:

1. Know Your Rights: Read labor laws, workplace policies, and national regulations.
2. Seek Legal Protection: Many countries have whistleblower protections for victims of harassment.

3. Go Public if Necessary: Some cases gain justice only through exposure and activism.
4. Join Support Networks: Women's organizations and legal aid groups can offer protection.
5. File a Lawsuit: If all else fails, take legal action.

Also, you need to understand that laws are your backbone. In Nigeria, the Violence Against Persons (Prohibition) Act (VAPP) 2015 covers harassment, while the U.S. Title VII lets victims file with the EEOC for gender-based mockery and more. In the UK, the Equality Act 2010 helps victims against workplace intimidation, while globally, the UN's SDG 5 and ILO Convention 190 offer frameworks, although enforcement varies.

"A woman who refuses to be silent is a woman who refuses to be powerless." – Prof. Sandra C. Duru.

Organizations That Support Women in Reporting Harassment

If local authorities fail to act, women can reach out to organizations that fight against harassment. Here are some key organizations:

Global Organizations

- UN Women: Provides resources on gender-based violence and legal rights.
- Human Rights Watch: Investigates and reports human rights abuses.
- Amnesty International: Supports victims of gender-based violence worldwide.
- ILO (International Labour Organization): Focuses on workplace harassment cases.

African Organizations

- WARDC (Women Advocates Research & Documentation Centre): Nigeria
- FIDA (International Federation of Women Lawyers): Kenya, Nigeria, Ghana, South Africa
- African Women's Development Fund (AWDF)
- Sonke Gender Justice: South Africa
- Legal Assistance Centre (LAC), the Namibia Diverse Women's Association (NDWA): Namibia

Case Studies: (Wo)men Who Reported, Were Falsely Accused, and Fought Back

Many (wo)men have risked everything while enduring false allegations, reporting harassment, and demanding justice. Their stories prove that change is possible when women refuse to be silent.

1. Prof. Sandra C. Duru vs. Corrupt Officials in Nigeria

- As Principal Consultant to the Police Service Commission and Standards Organization of Nigeria, Prof. Sandra faced intimidation and blacklisting after exposing corruption and harassment.
- Despite powerful men trying to silence her, she fought back, exposed them, and ensured their removal from office.
- Lesson: Speaking out is dangerous, but it is necessary for justice and change.

2. Joy Nunieh vs. Senator Godswill Akpabio

- The former senior female official reportedly accused Senator Godswill Akpabio of sexual harassment in Nigeria's Niger Delta Development Commission (NDDC) in 2020. Shockingly, though, none of her accusations have been substantiated with any proof or evidence to date. This is very similar to what Senator Natasha has now also done to at least two different men, including Reno Omokri, and sadly, her latest victim is the same person Joy falsely alleged against.

After firmly denying the allegations against him, the then Minister for Niger Delta Affairs, Godswill Akpabio, magnanimously decided to let the matter slide without litigation or recourse to the law. However, this seems to have come back to bite him now, as I am pretty sure Natasha would not have been bold enough to dare level these heinous false accusations of sexual harassment and human organs harvesting against him if he had severely dealt with Joy to the full extent of the law back in 2020.

It's never too late to reap the fruit of such despicable labor, though, as Senator Akpabio has reportedly approached the court to address this issue and clear his name. Hence, she must either prove her allegations beyond any iota of doubt or face the full wrath of the law. Mind you, some of her close confidants and friends have secretly reached out to intimate me of how she had confessed to them that no such thing ever happened. Reports also have it that Joy is somehow linked with Emmanuel Uduaghan, who is now married to Natasha, so this is bound to be quite interesting to watch.

• I urge every man reading this to never seek any other kind of settlement outside the full prosecution and enforcement of the law whenever any female plays the gender weaponization card against you. Always ensure that you demand to have thorough evidential and legal closure on any unsubstantiated weighty allegations leveled against you by anyone, especially by the opposite gender. You are human, too, and you also deserve to be protected and safe from every evil.

The weaponization of gender and the media, and spewing false allegations to destroy the lives of innocent men and women, must come to an end in this era, and I dare say that there is no better time to fight for and to do this than now.

- Lesson: Even high-ranking officials face harassment; nobody is immune!

Conclusion: Every Report is a Step Towards Justice!

Reporting harassment is not just about personal justice. It is about changing the system for future generations of women.

You're not alone. Report with confidence, and use HR, laws, or communities. Seek allies among your friends or groups that can back you. Demand change and continue to push for enforcement. This chapter is your battle plan. With courage and persistence, (wo)men can break the silence and win justice.

"When a corrupt system sees a fearless person rising, they panic. When that person knows their rights, they tremble. And when they stand firm, corruption falls!" – Prof. Sandra C. Duru.

The next chapter will focus on how women can empower themselves, support each other, and create lasting change in their communities.

The fight continues.

CHAPTER 5:

Empowerment Through Knowledge: Knowing Your Rights & Fighting Back

"An empowered woman is a dangerous woman; to those who thrive on oppression." – Prof. Sandra C. Duru.

Women and girls around the world, particularly in Africa, often do not know their rights when it comes to harassment, discrimination, and bullying. This knowledge gap makes them vulnerable to abuse and exploitation.

This chapter is a blueprint for self-defense; not just physically, but legally, socially, and psychologically. It will equip women with the knowledge, confidence, and strategies needed to stand up against oppression.

It is all about knowing your rights and fighting back, whether you're a man, woman, girl, or boy caught in this hidden war on (wo)men. Ignorance keeps us down, but understanding your power can set you free. So, let's dive in, arm ourselves with the tools to stand tall, and show the world what true resilience looks like.

Understanding Your Legal Rights: What Does the Law Say?

Many countries have laws against sexual harassment and discrimination, but these laws are often underutilized because women are not aware of them. **Knowledge isn't just facts; it is your shield and sword. When you know your rights, you stop being a target and start being a force. Hence, h**ere's what every woman should know:

International Legal Protections

Several global organizations and treaties protect women's rights:

• The UN Convention on the Elimination of All Forms of Discrimination Against Women (CEDAW): A global treaty that holds countries accountable for gender discrimination.
• The Universal Declaration of Human Rights: This recognizes freedom from harassment and discrimination as a fundamental human right.
• The International Labour Organization (ILO) Convention 190: Protects workers from violence and harassment in the workplace.

Key Legal Rights for Women in Africa

Laws vary across Africa, but some key legal protections include:

- Nigeria: The Violence Against Persons (Prohibition) Act (VAPP) criminalizes sexual harassment and gender-based violence.
- South Africa: The Sexual Offences Act criminalizes workplace harassment and assault.
- Kenya: The Sexual Offences Act protects against sexual harassment and provides legal recourse.
- Ghana: The Labour Act prohibits workplace discrimination based on gender.
- Namibia: The Combating of Rape Act 8 of 2000 shields against rape and is widely acclaimed in the country and Africa as one of the most progressive laws on crimes of rape.

"Laws exist to protect us, but they mean nothing if we do not use them." – Prof. Sandra C. Duru.

Self-Advocacy: How to Speak Up and Assert Your Rights

Rights vary by place, but the core is universal. In workplaces, policies like the U.S. Title VII or the UK Equality Act 2010 protect against gender-based harassment. Knowing your rights is not enough; you must also learn how to assert them. Here's how:

1. **Speak with Authority**

- When confronting an abuser or reporting harassment, use clear, direct language.

- Example: Instead of saying, "I don't like what you're doing," say, "This is harassment. It is illegal. Stop immediately."

2. Demand Written Documentation

- If an employer, school, or institution dismisses your complaint, ask for written confirmation of their decision.
- This puts pressure on them to act ethically and provides evidence for future legal action.

3. Use Social and Media Pressure

- Many powerful people only act when their reputation is at stake.
- If institutions refuse to act, go public. Use media, social networks, and advocacy groups to bring attention to the issue.

"People who know their rights are the system's greatest nightmare." – Prof. Sandra C. Duru.

The Power of a Community: (Wo)men Supporting (Wo)men

One of the most powerful tools against harassment is people standing together. (Wo)men who support each other create a shield of protection against bullying, intimidation, and abuse.

Unheard Screams: The Hidden War On (Wo)men

Ways (Wo)men Can Support Each Other:

• Believe and support victims: When a man or woman speaks up, stand with them instead of questioning their credibility.
• Create safe reporting networks: Establish women's and men's groups where victims can confidentially share their experiences and seek help.
• Mentor and empower younger people: Teach girls and boys how to identify and respond to harassment early.
• Refuse to participate in smear campaigns: Many powerful people use other (wo)men to attack whistleblowers, as Senator Natasha has incessantly done since I came forward to reveal her evil schemes and lies. Don't be their weapon.

While mentioning the importance of (wo)men supporting (wo)men here, though, it would be foolhardy of me as a woman, mother, sister, and female to fail also to implore every woman reading this to please do all you can to raise your female children and wards well: morally, mentally, physically, spiritually, psychologically, financially, and in every other way possible. Proverbs 22:6 - "Train up a child in the way that he should go; when he is old he will not depart from it."

A well-raised and well-groomed child can never be intimidated or easily enticed and then bought over with any bait dangled before them because they know they were raised differently from the corruption and filth that pervades the worldly systems around them.

Hence, they cease to be easy targets and victims for any evil person around them, and by that, you have truly been a woman supporting another woman.

It would also be hypocritical of me not to sound a solid note of warning to mischievous women and girls who seem to derive a level of demented pleasure in peddling false rape and sexual harassment accusations against innocent men. If women are to stand together, this kind of madness must cease by ensuring that anyone found guilty of such is severely punished according to the law, because such folly works against the genuinely molested girls and women when they come forward for help in society. Stop crying wolf when there is none; you are only working against other genuine victims of these crimes!

"The system wins when (wo)men fight each other instead of the real oppressors." – Prof. Sandra C. Duru.

Self-Defense: Protecting Yourself Physically and Mentally

While legal action is critical, women must also know how to physically and mentally protect themselves. However, knowing alone is not enough, so you must be ready to take decisive actions. Some of these include:

1. Basic Self-Defense Techniques

Every woman should learn simple self-defense moves to escape dangerous situations. Some basics include:

- The eye strike: Aim for the attacker's eyes with your fingers or keys.
- The groin kick: A strong kick to the groin can disable an attacker long enough to escape.
- The elbow strike: Use your elbow to strike the attacker's face or ribs if grabbed from behind.

2. Psychological Self-Defense

- Set firm boundaries: Do not tolerate inappropriate jokes, touching, or comments.
- Don't let fear control you: The more confident you are, the less likely you are to be targeted.
- Seek therapy or counseling if needed: Harassment can take an emotional toll, and seeking professional help is a sign of strength.

"You are not weak. You are not helpless. Learn to fight back." – Prof. Sandra C. Duru.

The Power of Knowledge: Educating the Next Generation

If we want a future where women are safe, we must start with the next generation. **Education is key.** Learn laws like Nigeria's VAPP or the U.S. EEOC process. You must also build networks and be persistent always. These steps turn knowledge into action!

What We Must Teach Young Girls:

1. Their rights: Girls must grow up knowing what is legal and what is not.
2. How to say NO: Teach them that they never owe a man their silence, obedience, or body.
3. How to report harassment: Girls should know how to seek help and whom to trust.
4. Financial independence: Financially stable Women are less likely to tolerate abuse.

What We Must Teach Young Boys:

1. Respect for women: Boys should learn that harassment is not masculinity; it is cowardice.

2. Consent is non-negotiable: No means no. Silence also means no.

3. Holding other men accountable: Real men call out other men when they harass women.

4. You must protect every woman around you: The woman was made for the man and not the other way around, so he must always look out for, nourish, nurture, protect, and provide for her as her head. According to the Scriptures,

she was removed from his most tender and delicate part (his ribs), and this, both spiritually and physically, implies that he must shield and protect her always like he would his own body (read Genesis 2:21-22).

5. Beware of Jezebels and Athaliahs: As much as you need to protect the females around you, you must also look out for yourself and be careful with the type of females you let into your space or get involved with. Some are masters of false accusations and fabricating evidence to destroy any man they target, just like Jezebel did to Naboth (read 1 Kings chapter 21). Avoid overly clingy and attention-seeking women who have zero moral, family, spiritual, and intellectual values because they are disasters waiting to happen. Female or male, every life is precious, so we all need to be protected by always being there for one another.

"Educate a girl, and she will protect herself. Educate a boy, and he will protect others." – Prof. Sandra C. Duru.

Conclusion: Knowledge is Power. Use It!

Empowerment begins with knowledge, and it also means using your rights actively. When a woman knows her rights, speaks up, and stands firm, she becomes unstoppable. However, a good woman never destroys, complicates, or sabotages things in the guise of standing up for herself or being firm. Instead, she is a great manager and administrator of anything entrusted into her hands.

As a woman, you must never forget that your true power is your femininity and uncompromised virtue, and not an arrogant, uncultured, uncontrolled, uncouth, and senselessly confrontational spirit. When a woman remains true to her God-given feminine nature, she will know how to play in the space of men, where she will not only stand out but also achieve excellent, unprecedented, and hitherto unthinkable feats.

For instance, for the first time in the history of democracy in Africa, and indeed the world, a country elected women as its top three officials: the President, Vice President, and Speaker of the National Assembly. On March 21, 2025, Her Excellency Ndemupelila Netumbo Nandi-Ndaitwah was sworn in as the 5th President of the Republic of Namibia, alongside Lucia Witbooi (Vice President) and Saara Kuugongelwa-Amadhila (National Assembly Speaker).

This unprecedented event further proves that there is no limit to what you can achieve when you stay true to yourself, your core values, your feminine nature, and your unrelenting yet virtuous spirit. All you need is the right information, great people in your circle, and a never-say-never attitude that firmly refuses to stay down whenever you're knocked down or face rejections in any form.

If Her Excellency Netumbo Nandi-Ndaitwah and her amazing team could pull this amazingly historical feat off, especially in an African country of all places, what would be your excuse for quitting or not going hard enough at your dream and vision?

This chapter has given you the tools to fight back legally, socially, and physically. **You're empowered now. Know your rights by studying local laws. Fight back by reporting, documenting, and persisting till you get your desired and deserved results. Support others by building alliances. This chapter is your launchpad. With knowledge, unity, and courage, you can surely win.**

In the next chapter, we will explore how to build lasting change: how (wo)men can turn their personal battles into global movements that shake the world.

"When one woman stands up, she inspires a thousand more to rise." – Prof. Sandra C. Duru.

The fight continues.

CHAPTER 6:

From Pain to Power: Turning Personal Battles into Global Change

"Every (wo)man who rises from the ashes of oppression lights a fire that will burn injustice to the ground." – Prof. Sandra C. Duru.

The battle against sexual harassment, discrimination, and bullying is not just personal; it is a global fight. When one (wo)man refuses to be silenced, they inspire others to do the same.

This chapter is about turning personal pain into a movement, about using our voices, experiences, and resilience to create lasting change. This is the crux of the matter, where men, women, girls, and boys take their scars and turn them into strength to change the world. Your story isn't just yours; it's a spark for something bigger.

So, let's dive in, celebrate resilience, and learn how to make a positive and lasting impact that will transcend generations after us.

The Power of Speaking Out: Changing Narratives

Unheard Screams: The Hidden War On (Wo)men

The world has normalized the suffering of (wo)men for far too long. Many people only recognize a problem when (wo)men refuse to be silent.

Pain can break us, but it can also build us. Every bruise, every silent tear, holds the potential to fuel change. Take Muthoni, a 24-year-old teacher in Kenya, who faced harassment from a colleague in 2023, for instance. The humiliation nearly broke her, but she channeled it into a school awareness campaign, reaching 500 students. Or consider James, a 29-year-old mechanic in South Africa, bullied for rejecting toxic masculinity at work. His pain drove him to start a men's support group in 2024, and this has now grown to over 50 members. These stories show that personal battles can ignite action.

Why Does Speaking Out Matter?

Pain isn't the end of your story, but the beginning of power when we refuse to stay silent. Hence, you must always speak out because:

- It breaks the cycle of silence and shame.
- It forces society to confront uncomfortable truths.
- It gives strength to other (wo)men who are too afraid to speak.
- It pressures institutions and governments to take action.

Women Who Spoke Out and Changed History:

- Tarana Burke (USA): Started the *#MeToo* movement, which led to a global reckoning on sexual harassment.
- Malala Yousafzai (Pakistan): Survived an assassination attempt for advocating girls' education and went on to win the Nobel Prize.
- Ngozi Okonjo-Iweala (Nigeria): Exposed corruption and political intimidation in Nigeria and became the first African woman to lead the WTO.
- Sandra C. Duru (Nigeria): Fought against workplace harassment, corruption, and bullying, despite facing blacklisting and threats.

These women prove that one voice can ignite a revolution.

"Women's voices are weapons. That's why oppressive systems work so hard to silence them." – Prof. Sandra C. Duru.

Creating Safe Spaces: Building Support Networks for Women

Many women suffer alone because they feel isolated. We must create spaces where women feel safe to share their experiences and support one another. Never talk down on a woman or victimize her for a crime against her that she has summoned the courage to come forward to report.

Unheard Screams: The Hidden War On (Wo)men

We must collectively work to put an end to the culture of victim-blaming when a female reports a case of rape or sexual harassment and shun the crude habit of passing derogatory and condemning remarks at the victims instead of comforting and assuring them of deserved justice if their allegations are genuine and verifiable.

How to Build a Support Network:

- Women's Empowerment Circles: Small groups where women share experiences, seek advice, and encourage each other.
- Online Communities: Social media groups dedicated to advocacy and support.
- Legal and Psychological Support Hubs: Organizations that provide free legal advice and counseling.
- Mentorship Programs: Experienced women guide and support younger women in navigating hostile environments.

"A strong woman stands alone. An unstoppable woman builds an army." – Prof. Sandra C. Duru.

Using Media and Technology as Weapons for Change

Social media and digital activism have changed the way people fight injustice. No longer can powerful persons hide behind systems of oppression. Their actions can now be exposed to the world in seconds.

How to Use Media for Advocacy:

1. Share Your Story: Personal stories are powerful tools of change.
2. Amplify Other People's Voices: Support and share the experiences of other women, men, girls, and boys.
3. Expose Corrupt Systems: Call out institutions that enable abuse.
4. Engage with Media Outlets: Use journalism to hold abusers accountable.
5. Start Digital Campaigns: Online petitions, hashtags, and video testimonies have brought down powerful predators.

Successful Digital Movements Led by Women:

- #MeToo (Global): A movement that exposed sexual predators in workplaces.
- #BringBackOurGirls (Nigeria): Raised global awareness about kidnapped schoolgirls.
- #SayHerName (USA): Highlighted violence against Black women.
- #StopRapeCulture (South Africa): A movement against gender-based violence.

"When men control the system, women must control the narrative." – Prof. Sandra C. Duru.

Holding Institutions and Leaders Accountable

Unheard Screams: The Hidden War On (Wo)men

Speaking out is not enough. We must demand action from those in power. (Wo)men must learn how to engage with legal, corporate, and political institutions to drive real change.

How to Demand Institutional Accountability:

- Petitions & Advocacy Letters: Demand policy changes within governments and organizations.
- Boycotts & Protests: Refuse to support businesses or institutions that protect abusers.
- Legal Action: File lawsuits or complaints against institutions that fail to protect women.
- Lobbying for Stronger Laws: Advocate for stricter penalties for harassers and enablers.

Examples of Women Who Fought the System and Won:

- Prof. Sandra C. Duru vs. Corrupt Nigerian Officials: Fought against harassment and intimidation, leading to the removal of abusers from office.
- Oprah Winfrey vs. Sexual Predators in Hollywood: Used her platform to amplify the voices of abuse survivors.

"If the system won't give us justice, we will force it to." – *Prof. Sandra C. Duru.*

Leadership and Political Power: Getting More Women into Decision-Making Roles

Change cannot happen if only men control leadership positions. More women must rise to positions of power in politics, business, and governance.

How Women Can Rise to Leadership:

1. Run for Political Office: Women must take leadership roles to influence policies.
2. Claim Corporate Positions: More women in executive roles means better workplace protections.
3. Start Advocacy Organizations: If the system is broken, build a new one.
4. Support Female Leaders: Women must vote for, mentor, and defend other women in leadership.

"A woman in power is not just a leader. She is a revolution!" – Prof. Sandra C. Duru.

Building a Legacy of Change

The fight against harassment, discrimination, gender weaponization, and bullying is not just for us; it is for the generations of women and men after us.

How to Leave a Legacy:

- Write Books and Share Knowledge: Document experiences so future (wo)men can learn.

- Train and Mentor Young Girls and Boys: Teach them early how to stand up for themselves.
- Create Scholarships and Opportunities for (Wo)men: Economic empowerment prevents exploitation.
- Pass Laws and Policies That Outlive You: Influence policy reforms that protect women and men for generations.

"The best revenge against oppression is not survival. It is forging a lasting legacy from your battles!" – Prof. Sandra C. Duru.

Conclusion: The Revolution Has Already Begun!

This chapter has shown how one woman's courage can spark a global movement. The battle for justice is ongoing, but we are no longer fighting alone.

"They tried to silence us. They failed. Now, we rise." – Prof. Sandra C. Duru.

The next five (5) chapters will be dedicated to a special case study on a prime case of gender weaponization and unheard screams that I was privileged to be deeply involved in, professionally and personally. It offers a perfect glimpse into the world of people who are falsely accused of sexual crimes, the despicable games, strategies, and lies that gender weaponization entails, and the exceptionally tough challenges any crusader of truth will face against such victimization and manipulation agents.

This is indeed a fight for all.

CHAPTER 7:

No One Is Immune From Unheard Screams: A Case Study On Senator Natasha vs. Senator Akpabio

"The burden of proof lies squarely on the one who makes the allegation." – Prof. Sandra C Duru.

On February 28, 2025, Nigeria and the rest of the world were rocked by a shocking report that quickly spread all over the media and shot up the trends charts on social media as well. A lawmaker representing the Kogi Central Senatorial District, Senator Natasha Hadiza Akpoti-Uduaghan, came out publicly to accuse the Senate President, Godswill Obot Akpabio, of sexual harassment and attempted intimidation, and subsequently proceeded to file a contempt charge against him.

From that moment on, things pretty much spiraled out of control, and an alarmingly shocking series of events began to unfold in which it was not only revealed that those allegations were maliciously false, but a more sinister and bigger plot was at play. This chapter introduces you to intricate details about the saga. It offers a glimpse into the harsh realities of people who are falsely accused of sexual crimes while also revealing the despicable games, strategies, and lies that gender weaponization entails.

Justice Or Vendetta: How It All Began

Was the cry of Senator Natasha a genuine appeal for help and justice or a well-orchestrated attempt to weaponize her femininity and perceived fragility as a woman against the Senate chieftain? According to reports, she refused to take her seat on February 20, 2025, during a Senate plenary session. Her rejection of the reassigned seat, designed to reflect recent party defections, escalated into a protest that disrupted proceedings, culminating in Senate President Akpabio reportedly ordering her removal from the chamber.

So, on February 25, 2025, the Nigerian Senate unanimously voted by voice to refer Senator Natasha to its Committee on Ethics, Privileges, and Public Petitions for disciplinary review over her conduct. Subsequently, during a televised interview on Arise TV on February 28, 2025, she publicly accused Senator Akpabio of sexual harassment, alleging that the incident took place on December 8, 2023, during a visit with her husband to Akpabio's residence in Uyo, Akwa Ibom State, Nigeria.

She accused him of maliciously picking on and victimizing her because she had rejected unwanted sexual advances from him. However, if you calmly x-ray even her accounts of this alleged sexual harassment, it leaves a lot to be desired and raises lingering questions.

Senator Natasha claims that she was **harassed by Senator Akpabio at his home during his birthday party on**

December 8, 2023, in the company of her husband and many other guests and dignitaries. The first question that sprang into my mind was how a man could harass you sexually in the presence and company of your husband, and he never attempted to defend your honor right there and then? That story reeks of falsehood and gives off a very strong "set up" vibe.

Surprisingly, she had gone online the day after the party and posted glowing praises about the same Akpabio while praying to be like him, so the question is: Why did she not say anything about it since it happened until February 28, 2025, almost a year and 3 months later, when she was reportedly called to order for her misconduct in the Senate?

According to a letter ascribed to Dr Olisa Agbakoba (SAN), the former Nigerian Bar Association (NBA) President and counsel to the Senate President, Senator Godswill Akpabio, made public on April 22, 2025, *"You claim that the sexual harassment occurred on 8th December 2023, but your allegation was not made until 28th February 2025; one year and two months later?*

Additionally, rather than take up this serious allegation that occurred on 8th December 2023, you were seen throughout 2024 at several legislative and non-legislative events (locally and internationally) with Senator Akpabio, your alleged harasser.

For example, you were seen together at the Inter-Parliamentary Union session in Geneva on the 24th and 25th of March 2024. In fact, you took several selfies and group photos with him during these events," Dr Agbakoba said. The Inter Parliamentary Union (IPU) held its 148th Assembly in Geneva, Switzerland, from March 23 to 27, 2024, at the International Conference Centre Geneva (CICG).

He added, *"Recall that in our first letter to you, dated 14th April 2025, we requested that you clarify contradictions in your sexual harassment allegation against our client, Senator Godswill Akpabio. Of note is the contradiction as to timeline and dates.*

You have failed to clarify your sexual harassment allegation on 8th December 2023 and your exaltation of Senator Akpabio on your social media accounts (Instagram and X/Twitter) on 9th December 2023, the day after you alleged he sexually harassed you. Rather than clarify this contradiction, you deleted the social media post, which to us is extremely concerning."

Was the timing of her public accusation a genuine attempt to finally seek justice or just a sinister attempt to weaponize her gender privileges to destroy the image and reputation of another innocent man?

You may also recall that when the news about her allegations against the Senate President broke, Reno Omokri, a former presidential aide to ex-President

Unheard Screams: The Hidden War On (Wo)men

Goodluck Jonathan, posted a video on his Facebook to recount how Senator Natasha had also accused him of sexual harassment on October 12, 2021, after they had a dispute on social media. In her false accusation against him, Natasha had alleged that she "rejected his silly advances" during a State dinner hosted by former President Goodluck Jonathan at the Aso Rock Villa's banquet hall during the reciprocated visit of Kenya's President Uhuru Kenyatta on May 6, 2014."

To counter and debunk her claim, Reno was compelled to post private travel details showing how he had been away on a presidential assignment to help mend the image of Nigeria following the mass abduction of the Chibok girls about one month before the dinner party, and was not even physically at the event where the alleged "sexual harassment" occurred. This proved that the allegations were baseless lies and he was clearly innocent.

Similar to what she has also done with Senator Akpabio, after the news went public that he wasn't even in the country during the State banquet, Senator Natasha hurriedly went back to her social media and deleted all her posts about the accusations, including a derogatory video she had made attacking Reno and his family, in an apparent bid to cover her tracks. According to Reno, he eventually decided to settle the matter out of court because he was paid "a hefty sum of money as damages" after she had gotten some "high-placed Christian clergy men" to intervene and plead on her behalf, with scriptural references to how Christians ought not to take one another to court."

He added that Natasha is a chronic liar, and *"The best predictor of future behavior is past behavior. So, before Nigerians crucify Senator Godswill Akpabio, I would encourage people like Oby Ezekwesili agitating for her now to ask Natasha Akpoti to take a lie detector test to prove her allegations. If I didn't have the flight ticket and my passport stamp and even videos and photographs of me in the State Department in Washington, DC, USA, and later at my son's school in San Francisco to prove that I wasn't in the country when I allegedly sexually harassed her, what would have become of me? Everybody would have believed I truly assaulted her, but she retracted her false allegations and deleted all traces of it online because I had evidence. It is Senator Akpabio's turn now."*

For a person as highly placed and in such a sensitive position in the government, this is a pretty disturbing trend and realization about Senator Natasha, and such gender weaponization tactics must be stopped, no matter who or how powerful or influential the perpetrators are!

"Manipulators, pathological liars, propagandists, and mischief-makers always have an expiration date, but so do the chances we're given to make things right." – Prof. Sandra C Duru.

Unheard Screams: The Hidden War On (Wo)men

A Sinister Plot Unveiled: The Truth Is Always Consistent; It Has Only One Version

As every well-meaning and concerned person initially believed, including myself, strongly thought, and publicly ran with, there was a possibility that Senator Natasha may have unearthed a terrible can of worms with her public disclosure, and also bravely put herself on the line to reveal many other cases of such abuse which had been unduly silenced and swept under the carpet.

As much as I had wanted to believe this and was ready to back her cause to the end initially, the soft, still voice of reason, fairness, and justice inside me never ceased to hum a tune of caution, and it was very soon vindicated. In an apparent but very misguided attempt to recruit me into her gender weaponization and malicious character assassination ring, I got a call from Senator Natasha in March 2025. The revelations she shockingly spilled were the end of my support for her cause and the beginning of my deeply harrowing journey into the world of the falsely accused who have no voice or means to prove their innocence and exonerate themselves.

While on that fateful call with me, Senator Natasha admitted to several atrocious things, but these first two were the proverbial last straws that broke my camel's back of support for her:

- She has no evidence to back up her allegations of

sexual harassment against the Senate President.

- She deliberately worked against the Senate Committee set up to verify and investigate her allegations against Senator Akpabio by sending a high-powered delegation of influential women and lawyers to disrupt the proceedings at the hearing.

She also brazenly made several other highly damaging criminal allegations, from assassination plots to human organ harvesting, with zero evidence against Senator Akpabio. So, at that point, I had to pause and ask myself: If this man, being maligned, maliciously assassinated, and attacked like this, were my son, brother, uncle, father, or husband, how would I feel? Would I stand by and watch while anyone decides to ruin any man in my life deliberately? I certainly wouldn't do such a thing then, so I decided to do what I do best in life: stand for the truth and fight for it to the end!

A little over a month after my conversation with her, and after I had made it clearly known to her and publicly that I would not be a party to the weaponization of the female gender and pushing false allegations against any man, I observed a hilarious switch in the approach and versions of the story that the embattled senator and her then-growing band of sinister aides started to voraciously spread all over social and traditional media outlets and channels. This did not move me one bit, though, and it still doesn't move me to date.

Senator Natasha initially publicly denied that she ever spoke with me and also claimed that she didn't know who I was. However, in her fast-becoming erratic and untruthful nature, she later came back to admit publicly that we spoke on the phone, but then moved on to claiming that her voice was cloned, that it was AI, and all manner of absurd lies and silly attempts to pervert the glaring truth.

The truth has only one version, though. Hence, it is always constant and can never be subdued or conquered by lies and deception. It may look like falsehood has the upper hand for so long, but you stay strong and keep your eyes on the truth because it will always prevail.

"You can't give what you don't have. And that's the plain truth! You cannot pour from an empty vessel, especially when that vessel is filled with deception. " – Prof. Sandra C Duru.

No One Is Immune To The Evil Of Unheard Screams: Even The Rich, Famous, And The High and Mighty!

Whether you are rich, high and mighty, influential, famous, or even think that you are the most beloved person in your locality, state, or country, the sad reality is that anyone can be intimidated, manipulated, blackmailed, and maliciously silenced till they're filled with unheard screams echoing in their heads but never to be heard by anyone else.

How can you guard against this and ensure that you don't become a victim of evil women and men who always seek to and take pleasure in destroying innocent lives?

- Never fail to take notes and keep detailed and accurate records of things, conversations, dealings, and people around you. You can never tell when they may come in handy.
- Please also do your best to have human witnesses who are credible and dependable and can always come through for you whenever you need them.
- As much as you can, always avoid putting yourself in compromising positions, situations, and places with anyone, no matter their age, gender, status, or creed.
- When in doubt about the integrity and intentions of whoever you're talking to or about to talk to, get your digital device or whatever you have on you that can suffice, and ensure that you record such conversations as much as you can. Never leave anything to chance because, if it comes down to their word against yours only, how do you prevail if

your assailant is more influential and resourceful than you are?

But for my astute nature and diligence in observing these rules and many more that I live by daily, it would have been almost impossible to help the world see that there is no iota of truth in all Senator Natasha was peddling against Senator Akpabio and some other men she singled out and targeted for reasons best known to her. Like I always love to say when I write to my avid readers worldwide, most of the time: *"Ana eji uche eme ihe – Wisdom is profitable to direct!"*

"The voices you permit in your vulnerable moments will either propel you into purpose or bury you in self-deception. Choose truth, not flattery." — Prof. Sandra C Duru.

The Demands For Law And Truth: Every Action Has Consequences!

The Federal Government of Nigeria formally filed a 3-count criminal charge against Senator Natasha Akpoti-Uduaghan for allegedly making criminally damaging allegations against the Senate President, Senator Godswill

Obot Akpabio, and former Kogi State Governor, Yahaya Adoza Bello.

Filed on May 15, 2025, under Charge No. CR/297/25 at the High Court of the Federal Capital Territory (FCT), Abuja, before Honourable Justice C. N. Oji, the three-count charge was brought by the Department of Public Prosecutions on behalf of the Honourable Attorney-General of the Federation.

The government accused Senator Akpoti-Uduaghan of making imputations intended to harm reputations, contrary to Section 391 of the Penal Code Law and punishable under Section 392 of the same law.

The first count centers on a televised interview granted by Senator Akpoti-Uduaghan on Channels Television's political programme, "Politics Today", aired on April 3, 2025. In the interview, the Senator accused the Senate President, Godswill Akpabio, of plotting her assassination in collaboration with former Governor Yahaya Bello.

Responding to a question from anchor Seun Okinbaloye, Akpoti-Uduaghan stated: "It was part of the meeting, the discussions that Akpabio had with Yahaya Bello that night, ehm... to eliminate me."

She further implied that the withdrawal of her official security details by the Senate upon her suspension was a deliberate plot to make her "vulnerable to attacks," suggesting an orchestrated attempt on her life. Prosecutors argue that these public statements were made with knowledge or reason to believe they would damage Senator Akpabio's reputation.

IN THE HIGH COURT OF THE FEDERAL CAPITAL TERRITORY
IN THE ABUJA JUDICIAL DIVISION
HOLDEN AT ABUJA.

CHARGE NO: CR/297/25

BETWEEN

FEDERAL REPUBLIC OF NIGERIA ………………………. COMPLAINANT

AND

SENATOR NATHASA H. AKPOTI-UDUAGHAN ………… DEFENDANT

INFORMATION

At the court session holding at Abuja on the…………………day of…………………2025, the High Court of the Federal Capital Territory Abuja is informed by the Honourable Attorney General of the Federation on behalf of the Federal Republic of Nigeria that you SENATOR NATHASA H. AKPOTI-UDUAGHAN are charged with the following offences.

COUNT ONE
STATEMENT OF OFFENCE
Making imputation knowing or having reason to believe that such imputation will harm the reputation of a person contrary to **Section 391 of the Penal Code Law, Cap 89 Laws of the Federation, 1990** and punishable under **Section 392 of the same Law.**

PARTICULARS OF OFFENCE
That on or about the 3rd day of April 2025, during a live studio interview programme "Politics Today" on Channels TV in Abuja, Federal Capital Territory, within the jurisdiction of this Honourable Court, You - SENATOR NATHASA H. AKPOTI-UDUAGHAN, made

Image 1

Unheard Screams: The Hidden War On Wo(men)

and you- SENATOR NATHASA H. AKPOTI-UDUAGHAN- know or have reason to believe that such imputations will harm the reputation of Yahaya Adoza Bello, (Former Governor of Kogi State).

COUNT THREE
STATEMENT OF OFFENCE
Making imputation knowing or having reason to believe that such imputation will harm the reputation of a person contrary to Section 391 of the Penal Code Law, Cap 89 Laws of the Federation, 199 and punishable under Section 392 of the same Law.

PARTICULARS OF OFFENCE
That on or about the 27th day of March 2025 during a two-w telephone conversation with one Sandra C. Duru, in Abuja, Fede

Capital Territory, within the jurisdiction of this Honourable Court, You - SENATOR NATHASA H. AKPOTI-UDUAGHAN, made the following imputation concerning Senator Godswill Obot Akpabio GCON to wit: *"...There was this popular, this girl that was killed, what's her name, umm Imoren Inlubong, that girl that was killed some years ago, that her organs were actually used for the wife, because the wife was really ill three years ago or so, when they killed the girl, and her organs were used for the wife..."* and you know or have reason to believe that such imputation will harm the reputation of Senator Godswill Obot Akpabio, GCON, President of the 10th Senate of the Federal Republic of Nigeria.

DATED THIS ...15th... DAY OF MAY 2025.

M.B. ABUBAK
(Direct
D.E. KAS
(ASSISTANT DIRECT
ADERONKE IM
(ASSISTANT CHIEF STATE COUN
A. A. KALTU
(ASSISTANT CHIEF STATE COUN
Department of Public Prosecutions of the Fede
For: The Honourable-General of the Feder
080799

Image 2

Image 1 & 2: *Copies of the 3-count charge brought by the Department of Public Prosecutions against Senator Natasha for her criminally damaging allegations against Senator Godswill Akabio and former Kogi State Governor, Yahaya Adoza Bello.*

The second count mirrors the first, on the imputation against Yahaya Bello, former Governor of Kogi State. Senator Akpoti-Uduaghan told the same television audience that a plan to assassinate her was not to be carried out in Abuja, but in Kogi State, under Bello's watch.

In her words: "A week and a few days later, when [Akpabio] met with [Bello], he then emphasized that I should be killed… I delayed going home because I had to put some measures on ground." She also claimed to have reported the threats to the Inspector General of Police and made efforts to inform security operatives.

The prosecution contends that these allegations, made on national television, not only tarnished the character of Yahaya Bello but also presented a grave national security concern, especially given the implications of political violence.

In a third charge, the Federal Government alleged that on March 27, 2025, during a telephone conversation with one Sandra C. Duru, Senator Akpoti-Uduaghan made a horrifying claim implicating Senate President Akpabio in an alleged killing and organ harvesting.

According to court documents, she stated: "There was this girl that was killed, what's her name, umm… Iniobong Umoren… her organs were actually used for [Akpabio's] wife, because the wife was really ill three years ago..."

This claim, referencing a real-life murder case that once shocked the nation, is now being legally framed as a malicious and unsubstantiated attack on Senator Akpabio's character, capable of inciting public outrage and diminishing public confidence in the leadership of the National Assembly.

The government maintains that Senator Akpoti-Uduaghan acted recklessly and with malicious intent, abusing her public platform to spread defamatory and inflammatory statements that have far-reaching consequences for national peace, security, and democratic integrity.

Senator Akpoti-Uduaghan was not in court during the first hearing as she refused service from bailiffs. Justice Orji, however, ordered that efforts should not be spared in ensuring that she is served before the next adjourned date in June 2025.

Conclusion: Who Do You Allow The Power To Speak Into Your Life When You Need The Naked, Raw, Unfiltered, And Life-Saving Truth?

Unheard Screams: The Hidden War On (Wo)men

Are you aware that many people perish, not because they lack opportunities, but because they consistently reject wise counsel and adamantly continue on their evil agenda and despicable ways? The case of Natasha reveals one of three tragic truths:

1. She may lack genuine voices that truly care for her growth, peace, and restoration.

2. She may be surrounded only by sycophants who don't love her but love what they can take from her, pushing her closer to destruction while mocking her behind her back.

3. Or she simply despises correction because she is too arrogant, manipulative, and unteachable to hear wisdom.

The tragedy of unteachable spirits is that they often learn through disgrace what they rejected in humility.

"Whoever remains stiff-necked after many rebukes will suddenly be destroyed without remedy." — Proverbs 29:1

And as I always say, the voices you permit in your vulnerable moments will either propel you into purpose or bury you in self-deception. Choose truth, not flattery, because manipulators, pathological liars, propagandists, and mischief-makers always have an expiration date, but so do the chances we're given to make things right.

As my late father wisely said, *"You can't give what you don't have."* And that's the plain truth!

Senator Natasha can never give what she has never possessed. She has no integrity, wisdom, evidence, truth, or peace to offer to anyone because you can only give what you have, and she, sadly, is void of any of these virtues.

You cannot pour from an empty vessel, especially when that vessel is filled with deception. Natasha is fantastic at deception!

"The tragedy of unteachable spirits is that they often learn through disgrace what they rejected in humility." – Prof. Sandra C Duru.

CHAPTER 8:

How Do The Manipulative Fight? Key Traits Of Gender-Based Propaganda, Manipulation, & Weaponization

*"Gullible people only read headlines and not the truth because **they're always motivated by greed and what to fill their bellies with.**" – Prof. Sandra C Duru.*

On May 1, 2025, the entire narrative of this saga took an unexpected turn in favor of the truth and justice when I, Prof. Sandra C Duru, went live on social media to make shocking revelations about the Senator Natasha vs Senator Akpabio case and also publicly make a firm declaration and stand for the truth no matter what it would take or cost me. The result? All hell broke loose!

Notwithstanding, from the reactions and all the gimmicks Senator Natasha and her well-financed but sadly terribly inept gang of "lie merchants" resorted to, I learned a lot about the way and mannerisms of manipulative, gender-based propaganda and gender weaponization agents. This chapter is dedicated to raising and sharing this awareness.

They Weaponize Ignorance And Naivety: Gullible People Read Headlines, Not The Truth!

One of the major reasons why the evil of gender weaponization, gender violence, manipulations, selective justice (if it could even be called justice), and the unheard screams of millions of women and men worldwide continue to linger is the dearth of knowledgeable, wise, dignified, and honorable people in the space and jurisdiction of these events.

This lack of intelligence, social awareness, and a healthy emotional and social quotient makes many involved in these matters gullible, culpable, and biased toward the victims they're supposed to be protecting. Sadly, this leads them to think with their bellies instead of their heads. Hence, these gullible people only read and react to headlines, propaganda, and sponsored mass opinions because they're motivated by greed and what to fill their bellies with instead of doing due diligence to uncover, maintain, stand on, and fight for the truth alone.

Otherwise, how else can you explain a crowd of supposedly literate and educated people publicly celebrating and jubilating that a person gravely indicted on severe criminal charges against her nation and humanity was humanely granted bail pending the next hearing of her criminal trial? Like, how gullible can you be to be celebrating being offered bail for a criminal offense you're on trial for?

Well, I believe the answer to this is simple and glaring enough: This isn't feminism. This is an elaborately Weaponized Gender Theatre featuring one actress, one script, and a recycled set of lies.

She once ran to me with a cooked-up tale of human organ harvesting, desperate for me to amplify it both locally and internationally, just like she tried to do with the journalist Usman Austin Okai and countless others. It is a calculated move to destroy reputations, families, and her country with lies dressed as advocacy, and sadly, this continues to thrive in Nigeria and every other country in the world because of gullible people who are about the truth but sensational headlines and plots.

However, the days of unchallenged propaganda are over. Such people must have no other option but to face the court and present their evidence, if they have any at all, because in the courtroom, gossip dies, and only facts survive.

When their lies and evil manipulations are publicly challenged, and they have no shred of evidence to support their vile accusations against the innocent, they go on an all-out attack on whoever dares to question them. They stop at nothing to subvert the law and truth.

No more gender weaponization against men!

"A shocking lack of intelligence and social awareness, and a healthy emotional and social quotient make many involved in gender weaponization, and false accusation matters gullible, culpable, and biased towards the victims they're supposed to be protecting." – Prof. Sandra C Duru.

They Weaponize The Media Through Propaganda.

One of the first things people like these set out to do is to pay as many major media outlets, bloggers, famous social media influencers, renowned journalists and broadcasters, and news organizations that they can brainwash and convince to work for them and be on their payroll. The aim of this is always to control the narrative and twist the story in their favor by destroying the truth and pushing their perverted agenda. In the case of Senator Natasha, she successfully convinced an elite lineup of seasoned media and societal icons who were gullible or greedy enough to fall for her lies.

From top social media influencers to TV stations, news platforms, bloggers, and an army of seemingly mindless online goons, she had her media manipulation game well thought out. Still, there was one thing none of them remembered. The truth never needs a crowd or sponsors to thrive because it is self-sufficient, self-sustaining, and can never be killed! Hence, armed with only my personal social media pages, I took on their entire machinery, never granted a single interview to any media outlet, and brought them all down by simply aligning and standing doggedly on that which can never be permanently silenced: The truth!

(1) Rufai Oseni and The Arise TV's Shocking Level of Propaganda Journalism

One of Nigeria's most prominent broadcasters recently made a fool of himself when he was exposed on live TV. How? After months of twisting narratives and supporting a pathological liar with ZERO evidence, he picked up his phone during their live show and, in his usual dramatic flair, he accidentally confirmed what I've been saying all along by finally admitting that he had realized that Senator Natasha's case was a criminal matter, and not civil.

Imagine a so-called broadcasting veteran who somehow refused to do any diligence by reading simple court documents before going on national TV and ending up celebrating a bail bond for someone being tried for criminal offenses. Such is the level and degree of mental manipulation they always try to put out subliminally. Yet, in this case, though, he and his cohorts at the TV station forgot that such wanton jubilations only further proved one thing: their principal has a case or cases against her, and she must prove her claims!

On June 19, 2025, the criminal trial of Senator Natasha Akpoti-Uduaghan finally commenced officially at the Federal Capital Territory High Court No. 8, Abuja, Nigeria, before the Honorable Justice C.N. Oji.

All the noise, propaganda, and social media distractions could not stop what justice had already set in motion. Not even the loud but empty theatrics of one of her most prominent aides, Dr. Oby Ezekwesili, who had shamelessly reduced herself to the embattled senator's memo-writing errand girl, could halt the weight of the law.

For the records:

•Case Title: Federal Republic of Nigeria vs. Senator Natasha Akpoti-Uduaghan

•Charge Number: CR/297/25

- Date of Arraignment: June 19, 2025

- Presiding Judge: Hon. Justice C.N. Oji

- Courtroom: FCT High Court No. 8

- Status: Defendant was formally arraigned and granted bail for ₦50 million (Fifty Million Naira), with the condition that a civil servant must stand surety, providing proof of landed property in Abuja.

This ceased to be social media noise or gossip and became her dreaded courtroom reality. And let me set the record straight once again: I, Dr. Sandra C. Duru, remain on the official witness list, and I stand ready to testify when the time comes. I do not fear liars. I do not flinch before manipulators. I do not negotiate with deceit.

While Natasha and her media machinery have been running wild with baseless accusations and gender-based propaganda, the Nigerian judicial system is doing its job fairly, lawfully, and with clarity. This is just the beginning.

(2) Reuben Abati And His Deliberately False Media Report

On June 16, 2025, erstwhile esteemed veteran journalist and media personality Reuben Abati published a totally misleading, false, and unfounded claim on his popular blog, claiming: *"Court rejects FG's request to arrest Natasha over defamation charge."*

This claim was a prime example of how those who seek to control the narratives in their favor will always go out of their way to mislead the gullible and uninformed public, and this happens everywhere in the world, too.

(3) Sahara Reporters' Public Dance Of Shame

On June 14, 2025, a keen observer on social media, Tajudeen Mayowa, publicly expressed his disgust and disappointment at another erstwhile credible media channel, Sahara Reporters' perceived complicity in this matter when they ran with an allegation targeted at reputation-damaging, cyberbullying, and intimidating me, a key witness in the case.

Tajudeen wrote: *"Even Sahara reporters of liars didn't even vet the document before publishing it. You can now see their journalists as beer parlour reporters, and the editor of the tabloid is incompetent because what they are after is to blackmail and tarnish people's image. Prof Mgbeke is an intelligent woman who knows her onions, and she always backs her claims with documentary evidence. She is the one who closed the mouth of the undistinguished senator who got to the Senate through the court and started misbehaving."*

His comments came after the media outlet had shockingly published an unverified, uninvestigated, and completely false allegation as part of the intense smear campaign against me titled: *"Nigerian Government Lists Woman 'Declared Wanted By Police Since 2016' As Witness To Testify Against Senator Natasha | Sahara Reporters."*

If only the so-called reporters from the Sahara had put integrity before their greed and bellies, they would have easily discovered that my so-called accuser failed to substantiate her allegations and never showed up in court because she knew and eventually admitted that her allegations were false and maliciously motivated.

(4) Oby Ezekwesili's Shameless Propaganda on Natasha's Arraignment

Formerly well renowned as a Nigerian economic policy expert and an advocate for transparency, accountability, good governance, and human capital development, it was both disheartening and shocking that a woman such as Dr. Obiageli (Oby) Ezekwesili could stoop so low to also engage in not only misleading but a masterclass in emotional blackmail, the height of foolishness, intellectual dishonesty, and dangerous propaganda.

She joined the female senator's circus wagon to shamelessly and consistently twist facts to suit their narrative, yet it crumbled before their very eyes. After boldly going online to accuse the Federal Government of Nigeria and President Bola Ahmed Tinubu of abuse of power for allowing a lawful criminal trial to begin, I took it upon myself yet again to foil her media manipulation by also going online to counter her and educate people.

An arraignment in a criminal trial is not persecution; it is due process. A court of law formally charged Senator Natasha Akpoti-Uduaghan with criminal defamation. That's not a political witch-hunt but the law responding to serious allegations, including false claims of human organ harvesting and weaponized lies designed to destroy homes, reputations, and institutions. He who alleges must prove, not parade in the media with emotional distractions.

It's truly shameful also to note that this same Ezekwesili Oby was part of the same delegation that Senator Natasha sent, with a petitioner from Kogi Central, Suberu Yakubu, his legal counsel, Dr Abiola Akinyode, the International Federation of Women Lawyers (FIDA Nigeria), and others, to deliberately disrupt the Senate Committee hearing on her sexual harassment allegations.

However, they're all acting like the victims now and pretending not to know that Senator Natasha privately admitted to me that the sexual harassment narrative was a deliberate ploy and her real target was to damage the Senate President and derail the National Assembly through sensationalism. She also revealed how she birthed the "Arise TV Female Award" and the human organ harvesting allegations against the Senate President. Oby and others allegedly advised Senator Natasha to deny that she had called me, yet their memo failed, their media noise failed, and then she switched to a sad show of performative outrage.

She brazenly accused the Nigerian government of abuse of power for allowing a criminal trial to begin, yet had no problem when Natasha tried to blackmail her way through institutions using false allegations, gender weaponization, and global smear campaigns. This is not advocacy; it is sabotage.

Let the world know the truth is on trial, and justice is finally taking its course. No amount of selective activism, media drama, or illogical outbursts from so-called advocates will change the fact that Senator Natasha has serious charges to answer in a court of law. And this time, there will be no hiding behind hashtags or rented crowds.

"The truth never needs a crowd or sponsors to thrive because it is self-sufficient, self-sustaining, and can never be killed!" – Prof. Sandra C Duru.

They Weaponize The Public Sentiment Through Emotional Manipulation

In the heat of the matter, Senator Natasha was reportedly caught on tape instigating a journalist in Nigeria named Usman Austin Okai to go public and incite the Nigerian people against the Senate President, Godswill Akpabio, by frivolously claiming that the Senate chieftain "is blackmailing" the President of the Federal Republic of Nigeria, Asiwaju Bola Ahmed Tinubu, and forcing him to sacrifice her, Natasha, or risk losing his support during the forthcoming 2027 general elections in Nigeria where the President would be seeking re-election for a second term in office. *"It's very important, my brother, please. Just be there for me so that Nigerians will come against them. Just help me, please. Thank you. God bless you,"* she was heard saying to him on the alarming recorded audio.

This is another classic example of how despicable people weaponize gender-based narratives to commit political terrorism and incite public distrust. Of course, she again came out publicly afterward to deny her involvement, retorting to her usual *"That's an AI"* and *"My voice was cloned"* lies.

While Usman Austin Okai may have his issues, the real question is: What exactly makes anyone believe that Senator Natasha, in her appalling desperation to impress some of her allegedly newly found allies and partners in mischief, blackmail, lies, and manipulation, wouldn't go as far as secretly recording her conversations just to gain their trust?

It has since been proven that she spoke to Okai, and the leaked voices and words are theirs, not cloned or AI, but their authentic voices. Hence, it raises another pressing question: Could it be that she was deliberately gathering these recordings as "proof" to convince them she had solid backing in Nigeria while plotting her dirty agenda abroad? Let's not forget how the public also heard her confessions in the leaked audio, where she openly talked about destroying me, Prof. Sandra Duru, and another principal witness in the case against her, the former Kogi State, Nigeria, Governor, Yahaya Adoza Bello.

So again, could it be that she leaked those recordings to showcase her so-called influence and credibility among her co-conspirators?

You may also recall that this same pattern was used during

the former President Goodluck Ebele Jonathan (GEJ) administration when this same Senator Natasha falsely accused popular Nigerian author, columnist, social media influencer, and former media aide to President Jonathan, Reno Omokri, of sexual harassment while Oby was chasing after the case of the then kidnapped Chibok girls.

For the record, I am not making any allegations or accusations here. Still, these similar series of events involving the same prime actors certainly raise valid questions in a logical mind: Could this be an opposition party's strategy to disrupt the ruling party? How come it is the same two women who were involved in the GEJ administration and with almost the same strategy, too: inciting the masses against the government with sensationally woven falsehood and weaponizing gender-based narratives to destroy notable men?

On another note, I would like to share this word of caution to people who cannot tolerate, accept, or withstand the same evilness and wickedness they freely dish out to others: Do not give what you cannot accept! Do you know that the same Natasha Akpoti who has been jumping from one media outlet to another and all over social media platforms sponsoring malice and smear campaigns against me and other people is now the one crying to the court to restrain me from exercising my rights to reply to her lies and trying so hard to stop me from exercising my rights to defend myself from her bullying, harassment, and sponsored attacks on my credibility, character, integrity, and reputation?

In the case with Suit No: FCT/HC/GWD/CV/229/2025, and Motion No: GWD/MI4510/25 between Senator Natasha Akpoti Uduaghani (Claimant and Applicant) and I, Sandra C. Duru, and Meta Platforms Inc (operator of Facebook and other social media platforms) as the defendants and respondents, she claims as follows:

- The Claimant|Applicant has suffered immense emotional distress, anxiety, and psychological harm as a result of the first Defendant and Respondent's defamatory publications.

- The Claimant|Applicant's family members, including her spouse and children, have also suffered emotional distress and embarrassment.

- That the Claimant|Applicant has been subjected to ridicule, mockery, and harassment both online and offline as a direct result of the first Defendant and Respondent's publications.

- That the Claimant|Applicant's professional relationships and standing in the Senate have been adversely affected.

- That the Claimant|Applicant has been forced to expend considerable time, energy, and resources responding to and addressing the false allegations made by the first Defendant and Respondent.

- That the ongoing nature of what she calls the first Defendant and Respondent's defamatory campaign has prevented the Claimant|Applicant from moving forward and has kept her in a constant state of stress and anxiety.

- Contrary to the allegations in the first Defendant and Respondent's counter affidavit, the defamatory publications have not ceased.

- That the first Defendant and Respondent continues to maintain, share, and promote defamatory content about the Claimant|Applicant on various social media platforms.

- That the first Defendant, between November 18 and 27, 2025, published defamatory posts about the Claimant|Applicant on the second Defendant's

Facebook platform. The posts are herein attached and marked as Exhibit E.

- That the first Defendant and Respondent continues to make live broadcasts and videos containing defamatory statements about the Claimant|Applicant.

- The previously published defamatory content remains accessible and continues to be viewed, shared, and commented upon by members of the public.

- That each day the defamatory content remains online, it causes fresh injury to the Claimant|Applicant's reputation.

IN THE HIGH COURT OF THE FEDERAL CAPITAL TERRITORY
IN THE ABUJA JUDICIAL DIVISION
HOLDEN AT ABUJA

MOTION NO: M/14510/2025

SUIT NO: FCT/HC/CV/229/2025

BETWEEN:

SENATOR NATASHA H. AKPOTI-UDUAGHAN — CLAIMANT/APPLICANT

AND

1. SANDRA C. DURU (aka Prof Mgbeke)
2. META PLATFORMS INC. — DEFENDANTS/RESPONDENTS
(Operator of Facebook and
Other social media platforms)

MOTION ON NOTICE FOR INTERLOCUTORY INJUNCTION

DATED THIS 6th DAY OF NOVEMBER, 2025.

Settled By:

Sunusi Musa, SAN
Michael Jonathan Numa, SAN
I. G. Kelubia, Esq
Aifuwa Imadegbelo, Esq (Signed)
Y.M Zakari, Esq
Odiyovwi O. Osusu Jnr, Esq
B. J. Tabal, Esq
Emmanuel C. Sogo, Esq
Q. M. Jim-Ogbolo, Esq
C. C. Eziukwu, Esq
(Applicant's Counsel)
M.J. Numa & Partners LLP
495 Adegboyega Atanda Street
Mabushi, FCT-Abuja.
+2347033740393
mj.numa@mjnuma.com
michaelnuma@nigerianbar.org

Image 3

Unheard Screams: The Hidden War On (Wo)men

> THIS DOCUMENT IS REFERRED TO AS EXHIBIT... A........
> M.J Numo & Partners LLP

Sen. (Barr.) Natasha H. Akpoti-Uduaghan
COMMITTEE ON DIASPORA & NGOs
COMMITTEE ON STEEL

4 June 2025

Meta Platforms, Inc. (Facebook Headquarters)
1601 Willow Road, Menlo Park,
California 94025, United States
Email: abuse@facebook.com

FORMAL COMPLAINT - CYBER-BULLING AND BLACKMAIL BY A FACEBOOK USER, WHO MAINTAINS TWO DIFFERENT ACCOUNTS IN THE NAMES OF "SANDRA C DURU" AND "PROF. MGBEKE"

I am Senator Natasha Akpoti-Uduaghan, a public servant and elected Senator of the Federal Republic of Nigeria, known for my tireless advocacy for human rights, especially in the areas of women and child rights, as well as transparent governance.

It is with deep concern that I write to formally report on Facebook a complaint regarding one of your platform users operating under two different accounts and in the names of "Sandra C Duru" (Facebook account ...) and "Prof. Mgbeke" (Facebook account ...) who has, in recent times, persistently used your platform and in the two different accounts to cyberbully, blackmail, malign my character and cause public incitement against my person.

In the course of my duties at the Senate of the National Assembly of Nigeria, it appears certain anti-democratic and anti-human rights elements have procured the said "Sandra C Duru" alias "Prof. Mgbeke," to carry out targeted online harassment against me. The said user has repeatedly used Facebook to cause public incitement against my person, post false, malicious, and defamatory content aimed at tarnishing my image, damaging my reputation, and causing personal distress. Her posts on the two accounts have amounted to:

- Character assassination and defamation
- Cyberstalking and coordinated harassment
- Dissemination of misleading and manipulated content
- Incitement of public hatred against ---

A few of Sandra C. Duru/Prof. Mgbeke' public and defamation of my person and o

I. https://www.facebook.com/share/v/1Ace
II. https://www.facebook.com/share/p/12H
III. https://www.facebook.com/share/p/14Jy
IV. https://www.facebook.com/share/p/1SM
V. https://www.facebook.com/share/v/14zg
vi. https://www.facebook.com/share/p/19As
VII. https://www.facebook.com/share/p/17t9
VIII. https://www.facebook.com/share/p/1A
IX. https://www.facebook.com/share/p/1Aph
X. https://www.facebook.com/share/p/16Gh8

Suite 2.03, Second Floor, New Senate Building, National Assembly
+234 8139819935.   senate

ACCELERATED PRODUCTION, APPROPRIATIONS, DIASPORA, MARINE TRANSPORT, NIGER DELTA DEVELOPMENT, COMMERCE
...

Unheard Screams: The Hidden War On (Wo)men

IN THE HIGH COURT OF THE FEDERAL CAPITAL TERRITORY
IN THE ABUJA JUDICIAL DIVISION
HOLDEN AT ABUJA

MOTION NO:

SUIT NO: FCT/HC/CV/229/2025

BETWEEN:

SENATOR NATASHA H. AKPOTI-UDUAGHAN — CLAIMANT/APPLICANT

AND

1. SANDRA C. DURU (aka Prof Mgbeke)
2. META PLATFORMS INC. — DEFENDANTS/RESPONDENTS
   (Operator of Facebook and
   Other social media platforms)

MOTION ON NOTICE FOR INTERLOCUTORY INJUNCTION

BROUGHT PURSUANT TO ORDER 30 RULES 1 AND 2 OF THE RULES OF THIS HONOURABLE COURT (2025), SECTION 6(6)(B) OF THE CONSTITUTION OF THE FEDERAL REPUBLIC OF NIGERIA 1999 (AS AMENDED), AND UNDER THE INHERENT JURISDICTION OF THIS HONOURABLE COURT

TAKE NOTICE that this Honourable Court will be moved on the _____ day of _____, 2025, at the hour of 9 o'clock in the forenoon or so soon thereafter as Counsel may be heard on behalf of the Claimant/Applicant praying this Honourable Court for the following orders:

1. **AN ORDER OF INTERLOCUTORY INJUNCTION** restraining the 1st Defendant, either by herself, her agents, privies, or howsoever called, from further publishing, posting, sharing, disseminating or promoting on Facebook or any social media platform, any material containing defamatory, scandalous, inciteful or injurious content against the Applicant pending the hearing and determination of the substantive suit.

2. **AN ORDER OF INTERLOCUTORY INJUNCTION** directing the 2nd Defendant to immediately take down and/or disable access to all offending publications, posts, or broadcasts made by the 1st Defendant against the Claimant/Applicant, whether in her personal name or pseudonym "Prof. Mgbeke", on its Facebook platform, pending the hearing and determination of the substantive suit.

MOTION ON NOTICE

Unheard Screams: The Hidden War On (Wo)men

IN THE HIGH COURT OF THE FEDERAL CAPITAL TERRITORY
IN THE ABUJA JUDICIAL DIVISION
HOLDEN AT ABUJA

MOTION NO:

SUIT NO: FCT/HC/CV/229/2025

BETWEEN:
SENATOR NATASHA H. AKPOTI-UDUAGHAN — CLAIMANT/APPLICANT

AND

1. SANDRA C. DURU (aka Prof. Mgbeke)
2. META PLATFORMS INC.
   (Operator of Facebook and
   Other social media platforms)

DEFENDANTS/RESPONDENTS

WRITTEN ADDRESS IN SUPPORT OF MOTION ON NOTICE FOR INTERLOCUTORY INJUNCTION

1.0 INTRODUCTION

1.1 May it please your Lordship, vide a Motion on Notice filed before this Honourable Court, the Claimant/Applicant seeks the exercise of your Lordship's equitable jurisdiction to preserve the subject matter of this suit and prevent the perpetuation of egregious harm against the Claimant/Applicant pending the final determination of the substantive action.

1.2 Specifically, our Motion prays for the following interlocutory reliefs:

i. **AN ORDER OF INTERLOCUTORY INJUNCTION** restraining the 1st Defendant/Respondent, either by herself, agents, privies, assigns or any person acting under her authority or instruction, from further publishing, posting, sharing, or causing to be disseminated in any form, manner, or platform whatsoever, including but not limited to Facebook, Instagram, WhatsApp, YouTube and other social media or digital outlets, any statements, videos, images or representations referring to the Claimant in defamatory, harassing or derogatory terms pending the hearing and determination of the substantive suit.

Image 6:

Image 3, 4, 5 & 6: Copies of Senator Natasha's affidavits and Interlocutory Injunctions against me and Meta (Facebook) where she demanded that Meta be compelled to delete all my posts and also restrict me from posting against her on social media.

Many other atrocious lies were dumped in her claims, but my lawyers and I have judiciously handled them all. Being the pathological liar, manipulator, and narcissist that she is, Senator Natasha again lied that she never called me and that it is not her voice on the recordings I've shared so far. Is that not confirmation that her brain needs to be checked by Adeola Fayehun after her abysmal outing on their show of shame?

Well, I am happy that she voluntarily admitted that she is "Lietasha." She claimed that she does not even know if I exist, that she never called and pleaded with me to join her propaganda against Senator Akpabio, yet she wakes up and sleeps on my social media platforms. The height of it is that she also shamelessly denied that she is facing criminal charges for giving false information to the police, even though the facts and information about the case are all out in the media.

I will not stop defending myself from her lies and attacks from all corners. Meta and my brilliant lawyers responded, and we won the first hearing against her in October 2025. She filed again in November 2025, and we also trashed her lies with the truth.

In their response before the High Court of the Federal Capital Territory in the Abuja Judicial Division, the 2nd Defendant, Meta Platforms Inc rejected her claims because my "publications can only be taken down if they violate Meta (Facebook) community rules." Hence, they urged the court to dismiss the senator's application for lack of merit, and also argued that restraining me would violate my fundamental right to freedom of expression and my right of reply. They also stated that I have already proven to the satisfaction of everyone that I have full justification for every publication on my timeline.

CT 50
E/R

**IN THE HIGH COURT OF THE FEDERAL CAPITAL TERRITORY
IN THE ABUJA JUDICIAL DIVISION
HOLDEN AT GWAGWALADA**

SUIT NO: FCT/HC/GWD/CV/229/2025
MOTION NO: GWD/M14510/25

BETWEEN:

SENATOR NATASHA AKPOTI-UDUAGHAN — CLAIMANT/APPLICANT

AND

1. **SANDRA C. DURU (aka PROF. MGBEKE)**
2. **META PLATFORMS INC.** — DEFENDANTS/RESPONDENTS
   (Operator of Facebook and Other social media platforms)

2ND DEFENDANT'S COUNTER-AFFIDAVIT IN OPPOSITION TO MOTION FOR INTERLOCUTORY INJUNCTION FILED 7TH NOVEMBER 2025

I, ADENIRAN HAASTRUP, of 11-21 Canal Reach, London, United Kingdom, do hereby **MAKE OATH** and **STATE** as follows:

1. I am Associate General Counsel Counsel, EMEA Disputes, duly authorised by the 2nd Defendant.

2. Unless otherwise stated, I am conversant with the facts stated in this counter-affidavit.

Unheard Screams: The Hidden War On (Wo)men

CHANDOS COURT HA7

SWORN TO at 11-21 Canal Reach, London N1C 4DB, England

This .17... day of .NOVEMBER......., 2025

DEPONENT

BEFORE ME

....

COMMISSIONER FOR OATHS/NOTARY PUBLIC

Notary Public London, England
(Edward Gardiner)

CHEESWRIGHTS
SCRIVENER NOTARIES / LLP
16 Eastcheap
London EC3M 1BD
T: +44 (0) 20 7623 9177
www.cheeswrights.com

TAYO OYETIBO LP

Image 8

Image 7 & 8: *Meta's Counter Affidavit in opposition to Interlocutory Injunction filed by Senator. Natasha Akpoti-Uduaghan.*

Still, she filed again on December 1, 2025, and even that did not go her way, as we again handled it brilliantly.

First, Natasha's lawyer applied to withdraw his earlier motion on notice for an interlocutory injunction, having already filed an amended one. As expected, we stood firm and immediately applied for a cost of ₦150,000, but the court awarded ₦30,000 in our favour. Well, there are no small victories, and every step forward is a sign that truth is already speaking for itself!

Subsequently, both parties adopted their respective arguments for and against the granting of the interlocutory injunction. We presented our case with clarity, truth, and the full strength of evidence on our side, and the court adjourned the matter to a date that will be communicated to all parties for the ruling.

I remain unshaken because the truth cannot be hidden! I am standing firm, and I am fighting with honour, truth, and divine backing. This battle will end in total victory, and I will certainly prevail against the Senate Crazy Parrot, who felt she had the monopoly of craziness to call a respected scholar with a pedigree like mine a "Facebook crazy woman," and then expect me to blow her a kiss. She must be delusional!

Do not ever mess with me if you do not have the time, energy, resources, brilliance, and the unique intelligence to match me squarely. I fiercely bring down the weight of my truth and the force of my evidence against evil manipulators and liars because I never lie against anyone, and I will never condone such from anyone.

"Think about it. The pattern is clear. The desperation is loud. And the betrayal is deliberate." - Prof. Sandra C Duru.

They Attempt To Weaponize The Law Against You: No Arm Is Without Its Bad Eggs!

Another very efficient tool that despicable manipulators and agents of gender weaponization and gender violence employ against the innocent and anyone who dares to stand against them is to use their wealth, power, position, influence, and connections to attempt to weaponize the law (the judiciary, police, and all) against them.

Sadly, there is no arm of the law that's not without its own set of corrupt officials who would not hesitate to throw the innocent under the bus and crush them as long as the price is right. These kinds go as far as engaging in targeted harassment, obstruction of justice by deliberately impeding investigations, physical and cyber bullying, and all sorts of organized evil against the innocent because they have been bought over and their consciences are dead.

(1) A Futile Attempt To Intimidate With Baseless Legal Suits And Claims

As mentioned earlier, Senator Natasha launched a series of vicious attacks against my integrity and public image in a deliberate effort to tarnish my reputation after I was named as the 4th principal witness for the Federal Government of Nigeria in their suit against her. Although all her plots and schemes consistently failed woefully, she relentlessly kept devising newer means to break me, and one of such was to attempt to use the judiciary to stifle and silence me.

After her initial suit in October 2025 failed miserably, she filed another suit against me on November 6, 2025, for exposing her lies, and demanded that I be stopped by Meta and not allowed to post about her anymore. According to her affidavit against me before the court, the senator claimed that I was cyber stalking and cyber bullying her, tarnishing her image by constantly making publications about her which are untrue and that these publications are done with malice with intent to reduce and injure her reputation as a mother, wife, and senator. She also filed that I should be stopped from making such publications about her on Facebook or elsewhere, that Facebook should not pull down all such publications done in the past and in the future, and I should be ordered to pay the sum of One Billion Naira (N1bn) to her as damages.

Unheard Screams: The Hidden War On (Wo)men

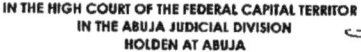

IN THE HIGH COURT OF THE FEDERAL CAPITAL TERRITORY
IN THE ABUJA JUDICIAL DIVISION
HOLDEN AT ABUJA

MOTION NO:

SUIT NO: FCT/HC/CV/229/20

BETWEEN:

SENATOR NATASHA H. AKPOTI-UDUAGHAN — CLAIMANT/APPLICANT

AND

1. SANDRA C. DURU (aka Prof. Mgbeke)
2. META PLATFORMS INC. — DEFENDANTS/RESPONDENTS
   (Operator of Facebook and
   Other social media platforms)

AFFIDAVIT IN SUPPORT OF MOTION ON NOTICE FOR INTERLOCUTORY INJUNCTION

I, SENATOR NATASHA AKPOTI-UDUAGHAN, Female, adult, Christian, Nigerian citizen of 3 Dala Street, Maitama, Abuja, Nigeria do make oath and states as follows:

1. That I am the Claimant/Applicant in this suit and by virtue of my position I conversant with the facts of this case.

2. Unless otherwise stated the facts to which I deposed are facts within my personal knowledge or obtained by me in the course of preparing this suit.

3. That I am a duly elected Senator of the Federal Republic of Nigeria and a prominent public figure known for national and international advocacy for human rights and good governance.

4. That the 1st Respondent, Sandra C. Duru, who currently resident in the United State of America using the Facebook accounts "Sandra C. Duru" and "Prof. Mgbeke," has repeatedly published numerous malicious, false, and defamatory statements against me.

5. That her last known address is No. 1 Chisholm Trail Road, Suite 450, Round Rock, TX 78681, United States of America.

Page 5

M J Numu & Partners LLP

MOTION ON NOTICE

Image 9: *Copy of Senator Natasha's suit against me where she demanded that I be barred from posting against her on social media, and be ordered to pay the sum of One Billion Naira (₦1bn) to her as damages.*

Unheard Screams: The Hidden War On (Wo)men

THIS DOCUMENT IS REFERRED TO AS EXHIBIT......
MJ Hamed & Partners LLP

Prof. Mgbeke's post

Prof. Mgbeke
15 October at 15:21

Natasha Akpoti Iro Files a Senseless Suit: Begs Court and Meta to Silence Prof. Sandra C. Duru Instead of Challenging the Facts

It is funny to hear that Natasha Akpoti Iro has sued me, Prof. Sandra Duru, only for me to find out that her so-called lawsuit is nothing but a plea begging the court and Meta to stop me from posting about her and to take down all my posts.

Walaih, I honestly expected Natasha to sue me for her voice and the facts I exposed. Why not challenge me that her voice was cloned, AI generated, or something meaningful?

So, she has the monopoly to drag people online without evidence, but now she is crying about being exposed with facts.

See her senseless suit. Lol.

Oloriburuku omo ale jaijati!

Prof. Mgbeke

Image 10

Unheard Screams: The Hidden War On (Wo)men

Image 11

Image 10 & 11: *Screenshots of some of the public posts I made in self defense, and to also keep the public updated about the matter on my Facebook account.*

Her case was split into two parts: the main case, which is the statement of claim where she asked for all the reliefs, including the ₦1bn damages, and an interlocutory injunction for the court to restrain me from publishing until the hearing and determination of the main suit.

In my response to her, I filed a counter affidavit in which I made it clear that I have absolutely nothing further to respond to in her display of recklessness and deliberate provocation. I am simply exercising my constitutional and legal rights to defend myself against her actions, false narratives, and sustained media attacks targeted at my person.

She does not possess the authority, moral, legal, or otherwise, to determine how, when, or for how long I choose to respond to the direct, indirect, and sponsored defamation campaigns she has initiated against me, my credibility, and my integrity. Hence, in my formal response, I wrote:

1. I, Prof. Sandra Duru, state in response to the affidavit filed by the claimant, Senator Natasha Akpoti Uduaghan, that the allegations contained therein are false, misleading, and deliberately designed to distort facts already before the public.

2. I admit that I made certain publications on Facebook and other media platforms concerning the claimant. However, these publications were made in good faith, in the exercise of my right to defend myself, and in response to a series of false and malicious publications sponsored by the claimant against me.

3. The claimant had earlier approached me with allegations against the President of the Senate. In my professional and ethical capacity, I requested verifiable evidence to substantiate her claims. She confessed that she had no evidence whatsoever to support the allegations; instead, she wanted me to join her already recruited group of women, as she mentioned to me, Dr. Oby Ezekwezili, FIDA, and Dr. Abiola, in her gender weaponization campaign against the Senate President, Dr. Godswill Akpabio. This confession shocked me deeply, considering the gravity of the claims she was making against a sitting public officer. She went on to claim that the Senate President is into human organ harvesting and how he bought his only son, how he killed one Ms. Umoren, and harvested her organs to save his dying wife, Mrs. Akpabio. I couldn't help but make an official statement/petition to the police, and that led to an investigation, and she was charged in court, and she has an ongoing criminal trial, and that made her

feel angry and called me a snitch, and all derogatory comments and harassment emanated from my bold step to expose her.

4. When I refused to participate in her propaganda or publish unverified claims, the claimant turned against me and initiated a smear campaign on social media and through paid bloggers. These publications labeled me a "fake professor," a "fugitive", a "scammer", a "crazy Facebook woman", a "wanted criminal", " bipolar", "mentally unstable and mentally deranged woman", a "school dropout," and other defamatory names, all aimed at destroying my academic, professional, and personal reputation. I was brutally attacked, including my reputation, character, integrity, and credibility, and none was spared! I lost customers, and my business collapsed! I am struggling to feed my three children as I am a single parent.

5. Furthermore, the claimant has falsely denied ever communicating or interacting with me, despite multiple pieces of evidence proving otherwise. She went further to claim that the recorded voices in circulation were not hers, but "AI-generated," thereby falsely accusing me of forgery and voice

cloning. These false claims were made publicly, painting me as a fraudster in the eyes of the public.

6. My publications were therefore a direct response to those malicious attacks, aimed at defending my integrity, restoring the truth, and enlightening the public on the dangers of gender manipulation, emotional deceit, and false narratives weaponized against innocent people.

7. The claimant has consistently used her gender and public position as tools of emotional blackmail and manipulation, weaponizing sympathy to shield her misconduct and mislead the public. My publications were not driven by malice but by necessity, truth, and self-defense.

8. The issues raised in her affidavit are essentially repetitions of the same falsehoods already addressed in my Statement of Claim. The facts remain that I acted only after the claimant's persistent defamation and public attacks against me.

9. I therefore state unequivocally that my publications were truthful, justified, and made in defense of my person, profession, and reputation, which the

claimant maliciously sought to destroy through falsehood and character assassination.

10. In conclusion, I acted within my constitutional right to freedom of expression and self-defense, and I stand by every publication I made as a necessary effort to expose deceit, protect my image, and educate the public on the dangers of weaponized gender manipulation and propaganda.

Subsequently, on October 16, 2025, I won the first round of the case she filed against me, and I continued to exercise my rights to defend myself. I also took firm steps to publicly make it clear that it is both unjust and hypocritical for her to employ media platforms as instruments of manipulation and coordinated smear campaigns, while attempting to silence my right to fair response and self-defense.

She cannot assault my name publicly and then dictate the boundaries of my reply. Equity demands clean hands, and if she cannot come to equity with clean hands, then she must face the natural consequences of her actions. My responses are not borne out of malice but out of necessity to defend my integrity, correct the falsehoods, and enlighten the public whom she has persistently misled through calculated deceit and gender weaponization.

She once mocked me as a "Facebook crazy woman," a "school dropout," and went further to sponsor numerous defamatory publications and smear campaigns against me. The same person was heard in recorded conversations instructing her associates, including Austin Okai, that she's using Adeola Fayehun and other media figures to malign my credibility, character, and professional reputation. She even directed that fabricated stories be circulated across blogs and online platforms to destroy my public image.

If she could call me a "serial blackmailer" and so many other derogatory names without remorse, then referring to her as the "Senate Parrot" is a fair, factual, and proportionate response. It is neither defamatory nor malicious; it is a justified reaction grounded in truth and lawful self-defense.

I will continue to uphold my right to respond factually, decently, and firmly until justice and truth prevail.

(2) The Nigerian Police Force Can Be Easily Manipulated Sometimes: This Must Be Stopped!

During the first few months of this shameful saga, it looked like I had the full backing of the Nigeria Police Force, especially with all the compelling and irrefutable evidence that I systematically presented as proof of all I revealed about Senator Natasha Akpoti-Uduaghan.

As the Head of the IGP Monitoring Unit, the lead officer assigned to investigate the case, CP Akin Fakorede, was initially full of praise for me, and he deeply commended my efforts to expose her lies and also protect the reputation of Nigeria. However, this tune eventually became a sour note in his mouth as he later turned around to start attacking my credibility, integrity, and character so that I would be removed as a principal witness from the case.

This same police officer started harassing, threatening, bullying, and calling me derogatory names to the extent that one of Senator Natasha's legislative aides, a certain Mr. Lamisi, made some false publications on his verified Facebook account, and credited the derogatory remarks and defamation used in them to CP Akin Fakorede.

The blatant compromise, corruption, abuse of authority/office got really bad as he kept threatening, coercing, bullying, harassing, and attempting to intimidate me, and I was forced to lodge a formal petition against him directly to the Inspector General of Police, IGP Kayode Egbetokun, and I duly attached all the evidence of my correspondence and exchanges with him to substantiate my plea against him.

Unheard Screams: The Hidden War On (Wo)men

Prof. Sandra Duru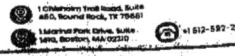

The Inspector General of Police
Nigeria Police Force
Nigeria Police Headquarters,
Louis Edet House,
Shehu Shagari Way,
Central Area, Abuja, Nigeria.

September 29, 2025.

Cc: Chairman, Police Service Commission
Cc: Commissioner, Police Service Commission
Cc: Chairman, Independent Corrupt Practices & Other Related Offences Commission (ICPC)

FORMAL DEMAND FOR IMMEDIATE REMOVAL AND INVESTIGATION OF COMPOL AKIN FAKOREDE, HEAD, IGP MONITORING UNIT

We hereby demand the immediate administrative suspension, removal, and comprehensive investigation of CP Akin Fakorede, Head of the IGP Monitoring Unit, on the following grounds:

1. Gross Misconduct and Abuse of Office: engaging in acts incompatible with the duties and ethics of the Nigeria Police Force.

2. Corruption and Malfeasance: deliberate abuse of power for personal gain, obstruction of justice, and compromise of lawful investigations.

3. Tampering with Evidence: deliberate interference with exhibits and case materials, thereby undermining due process.

4. Witness Intimidation and Harassment: persistent threats, coercion, and blackmail directed at a key witness in an ongoing investigation and prosecution, contrary to Section 97 of the Administration of Criminal Justice Act (ACJA) and international standards on witness protection.

5. Perverting the Course of Justice: acts calculated to obstruct, delay, or improperly influence criminal proceedings.

6. Violation of Professional Ethics and Oath of Office: conduct unbecoming of a police officer and contrary to the Police Act, the Code of Conduct for Law Enforcement Officers, and the Constitution of the Federal Republic of Nigeria.

www.mabeke.com   www.mabekevillagehut.com   www.tuffinc.org   www.wenetly.com

Image 12: *Copy of the formal petition directly submitted to the Nigerian Inspector General of Police, IGP Kayode Egbetokun, against CP Akin Fakorede. He blatantly dismissed it without due process in a disturbingly clear case of abuse of power.*

However, even with all the evidence submitted to IGP Egbetokun, the police boss chose to cover up for his erring officer and refused to call him to order or reprimand him for his unprofessional conduct, bullying, glaring abuse of office, and compromise. After reportedly reviewing my petition, the IGP shielded CP Fakorede, and said that I should "use my brilliance and intelligence positively," and that my petition against the CP "holds no substance!"

Seeing this height of negligence, impunity, lawlessness, and corruption in the Nigerian government and police, I chose to ignore all their gimmicks and instead responded to their continued harassment and malicious smear campaigns targeting my reputation with this affidavit in defense of my character, integrity, and personal rights:

"I, Prof. Sandra Duru, also known as Prof. Mgbeke, being of sound mind and lawful age, hereby solemnly affirm and declare as follows:

1. That I make this statement in good faith and in the lawful exercise of my constitutional rights to self-defense, truth, and protection of personal integrity, in response to the malicious, defamatory, and manipulative actions of the said individual whose continuous media attacks, false allegations, and orchestrated smear campaigns have caused

significant damage to my reputation, dignity, and emotional well-being.

2. That I have at no time instigated any act of provocation or defamation against her (Senator Natasha Akpoti-Uduaghan). My public responses are strictly reactive, factual, and necessary for the correction of false narratives and the protection of my good name.

3. That the said individual has, through both direct and indirect means, used media platforms, proxies, and associates to propagate falsehoods and defamatory content against me. It is on record that she referred to me as a "Facebook crazy woman," a "school dropout," and a "serial blackmailer." These statements were designed to malign my credibility, question my educational and professional background, and subject me to public ridicule.

4. That in a recorded conversation between her and one Austin Okai, she was clearly heard boasting of using media figures, including Adeola Fayehun and others, to execute targeted attacks on my integrity and reputation, and to circulate false publications across blogs and social media platforms.

5. That these coordinated media assaults constitute a deliberate act of character assassination, cyberbullying, and psychological harassment, with the intent to destroy my name and professional standing.

6. That my subsequent responses, statements, and clarifications, whether verbal or written, are legitimate exercises of my right to defend myself and to enlighten the public whom she has consistently misled through misinformation, emotional manipulation, and gender-based victimhood tactics.

7. That she cannot, under any law, moral code, or principle of natural justice, dictate the manner, timing, or duration of my lawful defense, having herself initiated and sustained a prolonged campaign of defamation, deceit, and public provocation.

8. That my reference to her as the "Senate Parrot" is a factual, non-defamatory expression made in fair comment and proportionate response to the multiple derogatory and slanderous names she has used against me.

9. That I maintain that my actions are guided by truth, justice, and the need to set the record straight, not

by hatred, vengeance, or personal animosity. I aim to uphold integrity and expose the calculated deceit and manipulation employed against me and every other unsuspecting victim.

10. That I hereby affirm that all statements contained herein are true and correct to the best of my knowledge, belief, and evidence available to me."

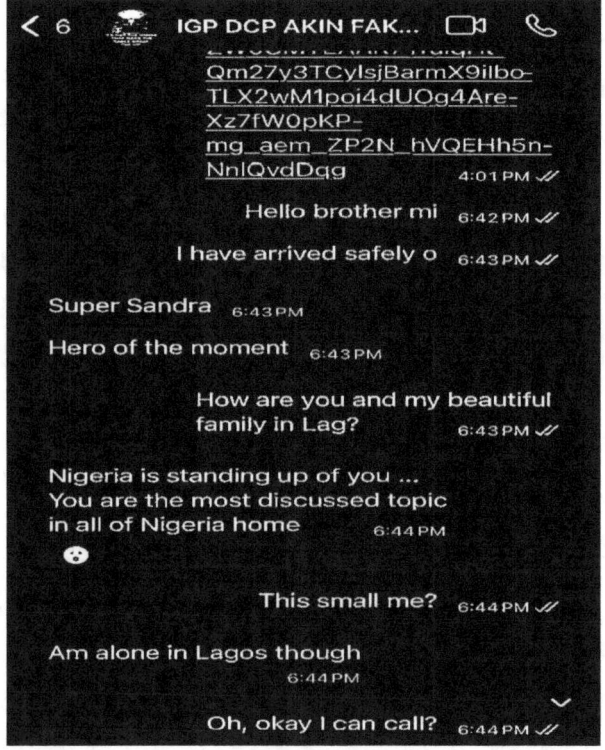

Image 13

Unheard Screams: The Hidden War On (Wo)men

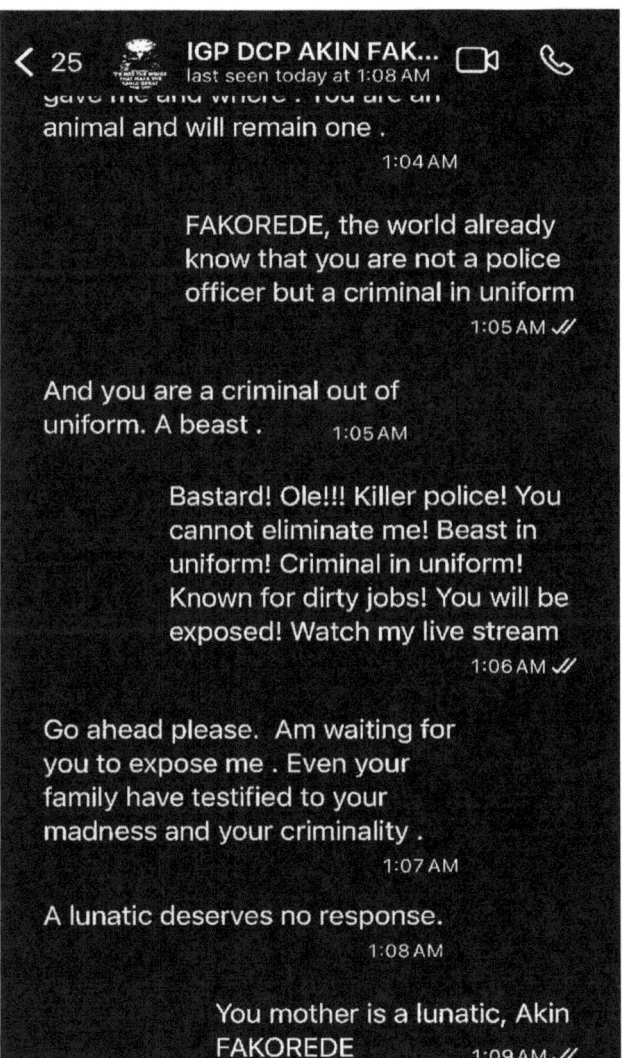

Image 14

Unheard Screams: The Hidden War On (Wo)men

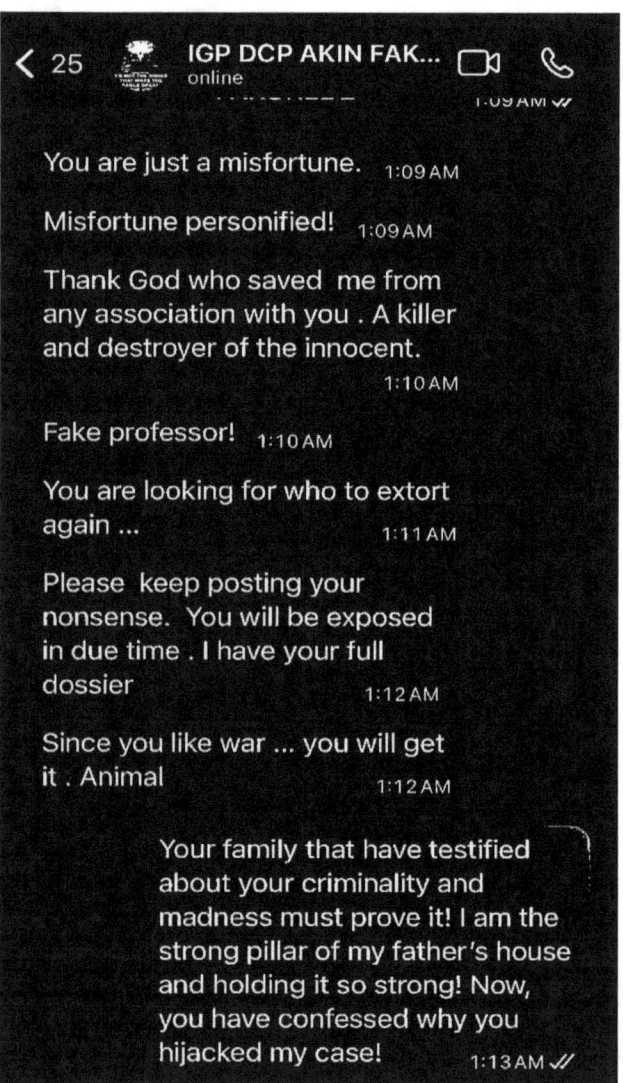

Image 15

Unheard Screams: The Hidden War On (Wo)men

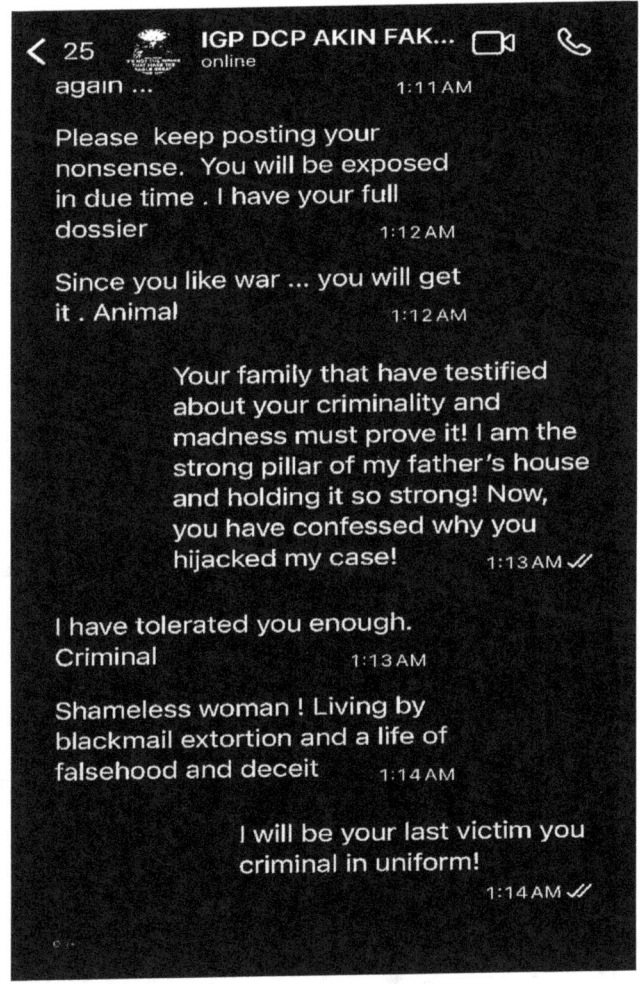

Image 16

Image 13, 14, 15 & 16: *Shameful and alarming direct messages filled with harassment, unprofessional, and derogatory words against me from the Head, IGP Monitoring Unit, CP Akin Fakorede.*

"Akpabio cautioned us to stay away from the mad, bipolar and illiterate Sandra" ~ DCP Fakorede (Head of IGP Monitoring Unit in charge of Senator Natasha's case)

DCP Fakorede: Akpabio declined appointment of Sandra Duru (Prof. Mgbeke), calls her deranged, mentally unstable person

Image 17: Senator Natasha's legislative aide, Hamza Lamisi's derogatory and publicly defaming Facebook posts against me on his verified account. He credited all his posts to CP Akin Fakorede.

Unheard Screams: The Hidden War On (Wo)men

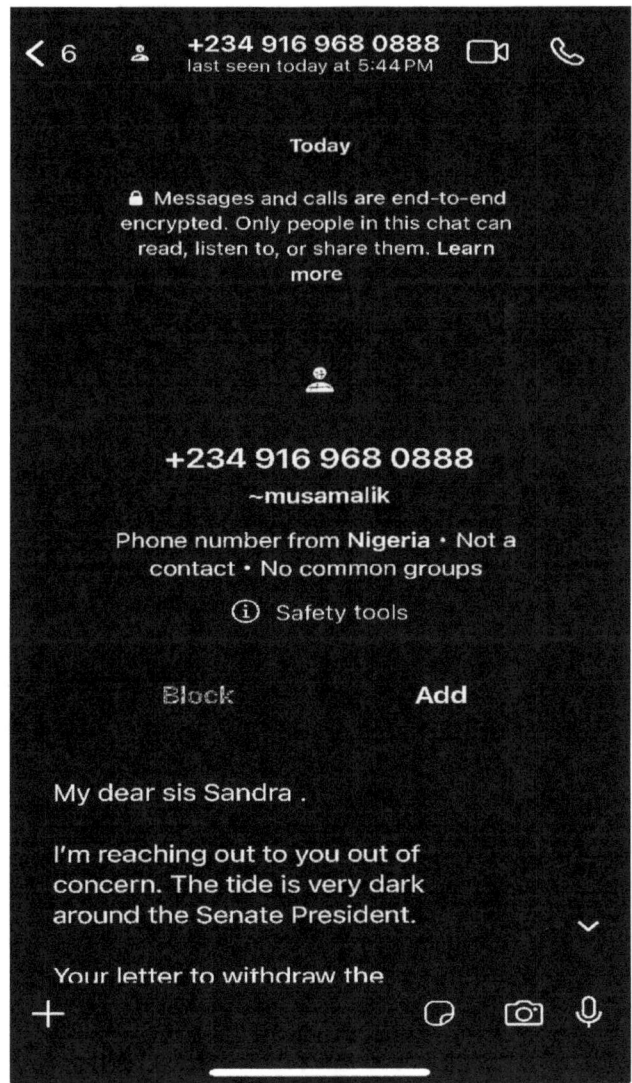

Image 18

Unheard Screams: The Hidden War On (Wo)men

> My dear sis Sandra .
>
> I'm reaching out to you out of concern. The tide is very dark around the Senate President.
>
> Your letter to withdraw the petition against Senator Natasha isn't going well with Akpabio and he is planning to kill you before you do so and expose him.
>
> Senator Asuquo has been sent to pacify you in U.K. DO NOT TRUST HIM.
>
> The IGP Kayode, SP's Akwa Ibom thugs and Asuquo's cult members have been notified and are conceiving plans to eliminate you even in America or wherever.
>
> Akpabio calls you a deranged and mentally unstable person; that's why he will not give you the appointment he promised and months ago cautioned all of us to stay away from the mad , bipolar and illiterate Sandra.

Image 19

Unheard Screams: The Hidden War On (Wo)men

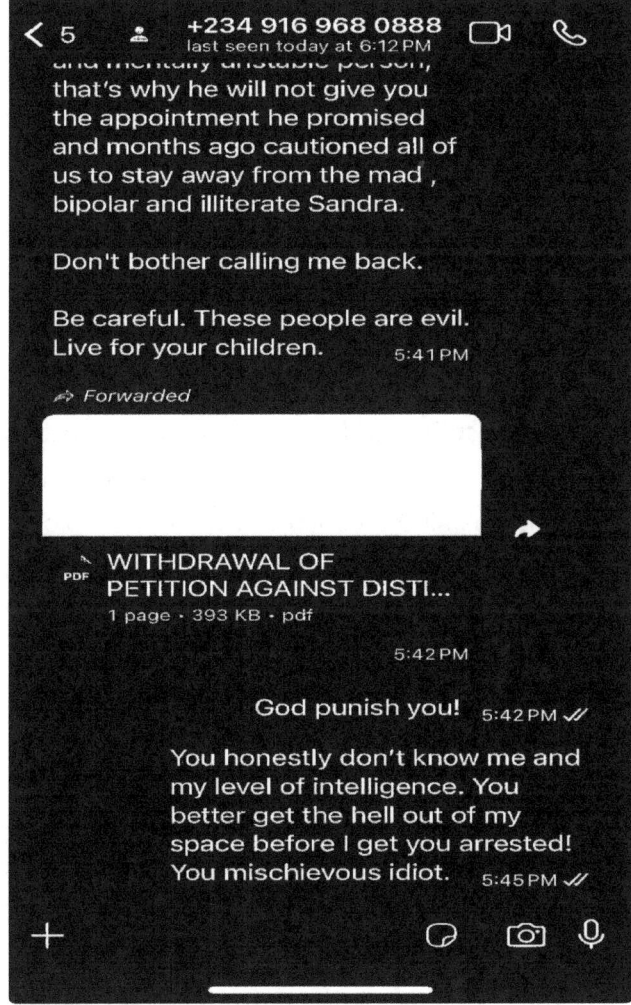

Image 20

Image 18, 19 & 20: Unsolicited direct messages to me from one of Senator Natasha's suspected cronies in attempted intimidation and harassment, with sutle threats to back off as a principal witness against the Senator.

Conclusion: Why Go On Mindless Attacks With Smear Campaigns & Baseless Lawsuits Instead Of Simply Presenting Concrete Evidence To Win Your Pending Case? Why Is Natasha Akpoti Crying?

In all of the exchanges that have lingered for months now between the embattled Senator Natasha, myself, and all her paid minions who have relentlessly attacked me from every angle and sphere of life, this particular question has always lingered in my mind: If the senator is truly innocent, and has all the concrete evidence to exornerate and clear her name, as she's bragged on several occasions, why isn't she presenting that to the courts against my alleged "false claims" about her?

Why is Senator Natasha only concerned and super bent on stifling my voice, infringing on my fundamental rights and freedom of expression? What is she so afraid of that has made her so desperate to have me removed from the list of principal witnesses against her in the Federal Government case against her at any cost? She goes about bragging that she has nothing to fear, yet she hasn't spared any resources and efforts to destroy my image and reputation globally in a bid to render my testimonies against her void. Why is she crying to every court in the land to silence me instead of presenting verifiable and irrefutable evidence to clear her name?

IN THE HIGH COURT OF THE FEDERAL CAPITAL TERRITORY
IN THE ABUJA JUDICIAL DIVISION
HOLDEN AT ABUJA

CHARGE NO:............................

BETWEEN

FEDERAL REPUBLIC OF NIGERIA .... COMPLAINANT

AND

SENATOR NATASHA H. AKPOTI-UDUAGHAN ....
DEFENDANT

LIST OF WITNESSES

S/N	NAME OF WITNESSES	DESCRIPTION	ADDRESS
1.	Senator Godswill Obot Akpabio.	Nominal complainant - He will testify to what he knows about the case.	No. 13 TY Danjuma Street Asokoro.
2.	Yahaya Adoza Bello.	He is also a nominal Complainant. He will testify to what he knows about the case.	No. 9 Benghazi Street, Wuse Zone 4.
3.	Senator Asuquo Ekpenyong	He will testify to what he knows about the case.	Senate Building, National Assembly Complex.
4.	Dr. Sandra C. Duru	She will testify to what she knows about the case.	1, Chrisholm Trail rd., Ste 450, Round Rock, TX 78681.
5.	ACP Maya Iliya	Investigating Officer – He is one of the officers who investigated the case, he will testify to the role he played in the investigation of the case.	IGP Monitoring Unit - Nigeria Police Force.
6.	SP Abdulhafiz Garba	Investigating Officer-He is one of the officers who investigated the case, he	IGP Monitoring Unit - Nigeria Police Force.

Image 21: The list of some verified principal witnesses for the Federal Government of Nigeria in the suit against Senator Natasha Akpoti. I am prominently mentioned as the 4th witness here.

These actions of hers constantly reminds me of one of my favourite scriptures in the Bible: "The wicked flee when no man pursueth: but the righteous are bold as a lion." – Proverbs 28:1. None of these events of the last couple of months would have occurred if she truly had any iota of evidence of her wild accusations against the Senate President, Godswill Akpabio, or any of all the maliciously acrimonious lies she has consistently spread against me. Even the government's case against her would have been, and can still be, struck out immediately, if she only had a shred of evidence to back up anything she has frivolously spilled against many innocent people involved in these cases.

Now the day of reckoning is upon her, but in her usual arrogance and alarming pride, she refuses to acknowledge the error of her evil ways and seek redress with the wisdom and favour the Almighty abundantly grants to any repentant soul who beseeches HIM for mercy. While she continues to try to bring me to disrepute, the truth that I resolutely stand for and all of creation will never cease to fight for me and bring all her machinations, schemes, and attacks to nothing. This is the will of the Creator, and nothing can ever invalidate it!

CHAPTER 9:

The Role Of The Law: How The Judicial System Affects Cases Like This

"Truth doesn't need noise; it needs time. And guess what? Time is here." – Prof. Sandra C Duru.

A lot has been said about the mannerisms and operations of people who take pleasure in destroying the lives of targeted, and most times, helpless, women, men, girls, and boys with gender weaponization and false sexual allegations. However, what role does the law play in all this?

How does the judicial system in every country affect and influence cases like this? And what can the law do to ensure that the innocent always get swift justice and adequate retributions are meted out to every proven offender? Let's see a few ways the judicial system can help and lessons from the court proceedings as things currently stand.

Education: Sensitize The People

During events leading to the eventual arraignment of Senator Natasha Akpoti-Uduaghan in court on June 19, 2025, many of her supporters took to social media to attack the President Asiwaju Bola Ahmed Tinubu's administration because they claimed that the Attorney General of the Federation (AGF) of Nigeria has nothing to do with Senator Natasha's matter and shouldn't be involved at all.

A high-profile criminal case involving very high-level officials of the country? This is both ludicrous and shockingly stupid, but it does reveal an alarming level of ignorance about the rule and workings of the law in society, and no nation should ever fold its arms and watch its citizens wallow in such.

Hence, let it be known to all that the judiciary never looks away from witness tampering, and, hopefully, it won't be different in this ongoing case because I am tirelessly working to erase all speculations and prove everything I know beyond any doubt. There are visual forensics, documented correspondences and proof, and confessional evidence, including this same Obinna's written confession, backed with media footages and financial trails, all in safekeeping to ensure that my case is water-tight.

A simple review of Adeola's interviews with Francess Ogbonnaya, Obinna, and Natasha Akpoti adds credence to all I've repeatedly stated: their actions are a maliciously targeted attempt to neutralize a prime witness in an ongoing criminal investigation, and they don't care how much money, media and social manipulation, and corrupt power they employ and expend to achieve their devilish aim. Unfortunately for them, though, with me, they are surely barking up the wrong tree.

The public needs to be aware and educated that this has never been about political rivalry, but about an appalling abuse of institutional lapses within Nigeria's security architecture, obstruction of justice, and a solid case study in criminal conspiracy. Everyone also needs to know that those who live this way recklessly will certainly reap the fruits of their wickedness one day, no matter how influential, connected, affluent, or powerful they believe they are.

That day of reckoning has come for Senator Natasha Akpoti-Uduaghan and all her cronies, and there is no power in hell great enough to deliver them from the impending justice because their judgment has been divinely arranged, signed, and sealed already.

Justice is coming, and it will not only be done, but it will be seen to be done by all!

"Every nation is only as good as the quality of its human capital: the people. Ignorance is a greater pandemic than AIDS, Ebola, COVID-19, and others combined!" – Prof. Sandra C Duru.

Bail Is Not Acquittal: It Is Not Victory!

The public celebration over Senator Natasha's bail at the court on June 19, 2025, was not only embarrassing, but it also exposed the disturbingly high level of ignorance plaguing her gullible and robotic noisemakers. It's just bail, not a final acquittal or victory!

After witnessing such a disheartening scenario, I've taken it upon myself to provide many others who may also not understand the concept of bail in a criminal proceeding with a quick legal education using the current case study.

Senator Natasha recklessly made several criminal allegations, from assassination plots to human organ harvesting, with zero evidence. These weren't just rumors; official petitions were filed, investigations were launched, parties (including her) were invited, thoroughly interrogated, and based on findings, the Nigerian government initiated criminal proceedings.

Based on the findings of these thorough judicial processes, she was formally arraigned in court, and not even the lies, threats, sponsored tantrums, attempted media and social manipulations, or Oby Ezekwesili's embarrassing memos could stop it.

Yes, she was granted bail, which is her right under the law, but this is just the beginning.

For those who do not understand how a criminal trial unfolds, here's a summary of what to expect: Such judicial processes begin with a hearing, cross-examination, witness testimony, submission of evidence, forensic analysis, and eventually, a judgment. This is not a movie. It is real-life justice in motion.

On my part, the puzzle became clearer for me in court that day because, unsurprisingly, Imo State, Nigeria, was well represented as the very man who reportedly linked Maazi Obinna Akuwudike and Francess Ogbonnaya with Emmanuel Uduaghan and Natasha Akpoti to be paid and positioned to defame the Nigerian government and me criminally, showed his face.

So, instead of popping champagne over bail, maybe study the remaining charges and prepare yourself for what is yet to come because the storm of justice is indeed coming, and no guilty party shall ever be spared the wrath of the law!

After being arrested and subsequently released on bail for his major role in the vicious attacks against my name, life, family, brand, and well-being, Obinna Akuwudike also displayed an acute lack of gumption, tact, and "common sense" as he regained his access to the internet by going on another tirade against me, howbeit subtle like the snake he is.

What he didn't realize was that his attempt to malign and maliciously mock me again was a complete blessing in disguise for me because, in one fell swoop, he unmasked all the "masquerades" still parading as friends around me.

He reeled out a long list of names, and I must confess that I am amused at his tactless reasoning because he literally handed me a comprehensive list of people to keep at arm's length forever, and also highlighted the roles they've all played against me.

While also seemingly forgetting that being out on bail is nothing compared to being discharged and acquitted, Obinna continued from where he stopped in the service of his pay masters before his arrest. Apparently, no one in their camp is smart or knowledgeable enough to know that harassing, threatening, or attempting to intimidate, harm, or manipulate a principal witness in any criminal investigation is a felony punishable under both Nigerian and international criminal procedure laws. Obstructing justice and undermining the integrity of a judicial process through defamation, intimidation, coercion, or attempted bribery of such a witness, as I am in the case against Senator Natasha, is a punishable crime.

His play-acting and "crying wolf" are all ploys to induce public support and sympathy, and also to cast me in a bad light by falsely implying that he is being threatened or targeted. This barrage of unending lies and deception is an apparent part of his entire being, yet he was so fluent in referring to and calling upon the name of the Almighty God on several occasions in his posts. Still, he forgets that the one he's referring to is not a man, nor is he given to the same folly, treachery, and bile that pervades the thoughts of his kind.

The great Apostle Paul warned the Church in Galatia: "Be not deceived; God is not mocked: for whatsoever a man soweth, that shall he also reap." – Galatians 6:7. Obinna thinks he can outsmart God, though, by being mischievously evil in secret but coming before the public to "lift holy hands" as if he were innocent. He will, very soon, learn that all who have tried such folly before him met with deservingly disastrous ends, and I dare to say that his own will not be any different if he continues on his chosen evil path.

Thank you, Obinna, for exposing your entire team of wicked co-conspirators, including the top masterminds, Eze Madumere and Prof Chinedu Asinu-Anosike (Cona), and others like Barr. Mrs. Vivian Ottih, Bemi, Dr. Collins Ugorji, Ezinne Precious and Deaconess, MamaPee, Precious Iluo-oghene, Mr. Common Sense, Chidiebube Okeoma, Jones Fcc Onwuasoanya, Igboayaka O Igboayaka, Sowore Omoyele's Sahara Reporters, Nwamah Chisomaga, Darlington Irobi Darlington, Daniel Opara, Don Peace

Nwachukwu, Angus Godwin Angus, Romanus Obinna Ukwunna, and, of course, his principals, Senator Natasha Akpoti-Uduaghan and her husband, Emmanuel Uduaghan, and others.

Do not worry; it is called the *"long arm of the law"* for a reason, and every one of you is going to grasp the meaning sooner rather than later. Yes, the tortoise is always mocked for its speed, but do you know that it always outlives its mockers? Obinna drank from my well, wiped his mouth, and then spat into it, forgetting that the same ground he's trampling today will be his bed when the wind of justice blows.

I was good to him and his family, not because he deserved it, but because my spirit is seasoned with grace. Yet, he rudely betrayed me, thinking he was smart, but he forgets that the palm wine tapper knows which tree gives the sweetest sap, yet he lets the sour one ferment. He and all who stand with him in their gender weaponization and malicious evil will surely remember me when their hearts inevitably start to taste their own poison. He may rise now with very weak borrowed wings, but he will surely land with his own legs, and his back must touch the ground.

And to all the gullible and hungry choir of confusion chanting *"contempt"* and *"imprisonment"* over Obinna's lawful arrest and detention without the faintest grasp of legal procedure or constitutional rights, I could take the time to educate you on the principles of law, criminal justice, human rights, privacy, and the ethics of public communication. However, I'll reserve that lecture for the right forum where the chess masters of gender weaponization and manipulation sit. At the appointed time, I'll educate all of you methodically, as a trained pedagogue, not a participant in noise.

"Whoso diggeth a pit shall fall therein: and he that rolleth a stone, it will return upon him." – Proverbs 26:27. As for me, I will never kneel or bow before betrayal; I stand, unshaken, and divinely backed. The Lord has spoken, and those who dig graves for the innocent always fall in. Keep watching. The battle line is drawn, and *Victoria Ascerta*!

"The meeting will be in court. The evidence will speak, and justice will roll like a river, unhindered, unbiased, and undeniable!" – Prof. Sandra C Duru.

Arraignment Is Not For Celebration: It Is Not "Natasha Day!"

Another reason why every nation's judicial system cannot afford to allow its people to continue in wanton ignorance of the law and its processes is that manipulative people are always quick to deploy propaganda they deviously spin into pity-party parades. So, let's set the record straight.

June 19, 2025, was never "Natasha Day." It was the court-appointed date for the criminal arraignment of Senator Natasha Akpoti-Uduaghan, following serious allegations ranging from false claims of assassination attempts to human organ harvesting conspiracies and other grave infractions against the state and individuals. The court never staged a theater for emotion but executed its constitutional duty to deliver justice based on law and facts, not manipulated sentiments or gender camouflage.

Twisting this clear legal process into a "fight for girls" is not just desperately deceptive but highly dangerous. That hearing wasn't about gender justice; it was about justice, period! Women's issues are real and important. However, weaponizing womanhood to deflect from criminal accountability is an insult to every woman fighting real battles against oppression.

Even more annoying were the inciting posts that went on her behalf that day, which were quite foolish, uninformed, yet cunning at the same time. Attempts were made to mix the trauma of the Chibok and Dapchi girls, true national tragedies, with the courtroom appearance of a woman being called to answer for her actions. That's not activism; that's manipulative madness!

No one is "coming after" anyone. A person accused of a crime is expected to face the law, just like everyone else. Hence, Senator Natasha's day in court was not persecution; it was due process. If she's innocent, she will prove it there, not on Instagram with hashtags and false analogies.

So do not be misled. This is not a battle cry; it's a reckoning. And justice is watching.

An Unsealed Office Is Not An Exoneration: Wake Up!

After serving out her six-month suspension from the Nigerian Senate, Senator Natasha's office at the National Assembly building in Abuja, Nigeria, was unsealed on September 23, 2025, and the reactions that followed from her alarmingly ignorant loyalists couldn't help but make me genuinely wonder about their level of intelligence.

Just because an office was unsealed after six months, suddenly there was jubilation, with ludicrous insults hurled at the Senate, its leadership, and even Nigeria itself. Suddenly, she started to be hailed as powerful, strong, unapologetic, and a lion who had "defeated them all." Some even claimed that the Nigerian Senate was afraid, and that their official resumption was postponed because of her. Honestly, I couldn't help but laugh at the sheer gullibility.

None of them can read between the lines, so I feel it is on me to make this very clear once again: this is only the beginning. The sexual harassment case hasn't been decided. Every allegation she made, and every false claim, has yet to be treated. Even the organ harvesting and the criminal defamation cases have not been proven or even concluded, yet her people celebrate as if all has been resolved.

Does an unsealed office now erase crimes? Does it cancel ongoing criminal investigations or trials? Does it prevent future ones? Does it exempt her from following the rules, regulations, and ethics governing her position in the Senate? Absolutely not.

Wake up. Think. This is not about education alone. It is about the ability to process, analyze, evaluate, and understand law and procedure. Sadly, many people in this generation seem to have neither sense nor judgment, and they've chosen to remain gullible, hungry, senseless, uninformed, and ignorant of law and ethics.

Natasha may be unapologetic, indisciplined, or unruly, but that does not translate into power over Nigeria, over institutions, or over the rule of law. Opening a door to a child who caused a crisis does not erase the fact that the child broke the rules. The principle is the same here.

This is just the beginning. Evidence must be presented. Cases must be proven. Laws must be upheld. Stop the hero worship and blind admiration. Get wise, get educated, and stop embarrassing yourself and your country!

"Now it is time for cross-examination, not cross-dressing the truth. No more hiding behind fake activism and memo terrorism. Let justice roll on like a river, and righteousness like a never-failing stream." – Prof. Sandra C Duru.

CHAPTER 10:

Food For Deep Thoughts: Is There A Link Between Social Manipulation & National Security?

"This is not just politics. This is a threat to democracy, to law and order, and the sovereignty of the Nigerian state." – Prof. Sandra C Duru.

Ever since the beginning of this ugly and deeply disturbing case that has brought undue and unwanted negative attention to Nigeria, her people, and leadership, there have been some pretty interesting and intelligent discourses and questions put forward by well-meaning Nigerians and observers online.

These questions and theories are in no way accusations against anyone, nor are they intended to be; either directly or by inference. Still, they hold some pretty valid food for deep thoughts, and here are a few below.

Social Manipulation And Engineering: A Needless Distraction Or Bigger Threat?

Whenever a person or group of persons deliberately sets out to create discord within a people or nation by inciting them against one another, can such social engineering and manipulation of people continue to be viewed as just a needless distraction, or should it be rightly considered as a bigger threat?

Hence, to those asking how much of a security threat Senator Natasha and her cohorts are, and even reportedly relating it to what happened in Benue State, Nigeria, on June 13, 2025, I would like to ask: How did *"bring back our girls"* start?

This is a valid concern, and anyone asking is absolutely right to point out what's happening in Benue because those recurring attacks are heartbreaking and should never be normalized. But here's the thing: security threats aren't limited to one region or one form. The patterns we see in the leaked audio, including calculated disruptions and manipulation of public sentiment, are also valid national security concerns.

They may not come with bullets, but they aim to destabilize governance, incite division, and compromise the nation's unity from within. Benue is bleeding physically, and this other side is bleeding our systems and minds. Both must be tackled simultaneously and seriously.

"A threat to one part of Nigeria is a threat to all. Let's not treat any of them lightly." - Prof. Sandra C Duru.

Real Enemies Or Mere Coincidences: Are These Acts Enough For A National Security Alert?

As I continued to x-ray many elements interwoven into this particular dynamic case study, I sincerely could not rid myself of these burning questions: Who are the real enemies of the nation, and are these actions enough to raise a national security alert?

I reiterate that these are by no means direct accusations against anyone or a group of persons, but valid facts that I firmly believe we should think deeply about and take appropriate steps if needed, before things totally spiral out of control.

When patterns repeat in calculated cycles, it's no longer a mere coincidence; it is a strategy. This is not just a call for observation. This is a call for national attention. A dangerous narrative is unfolding beneath the surface, and the signs have become too clear to ignore.

Let's begin with the allegedly leaked audio involving Natasha Akpoti-Uduaghan. In this chilling exposé, she reportedly brags about orchestrating deliberate disruptions to federal committee proceedings by mobilizing high-profile individuals, including the International Federation of Women Lawyers (FIDA Nigeria), Dr. Oby Ezekwesili, Suberu Yakubu, and Dr Abiola Akinyode. These weren't acts of advocacy; they were coordinated interferences designed to delay justice, manipulate public sentiment, and derail governmental processes.

Who empowered her to wield such influence over key civil society actors and legal stakeholders? And more importantly, to what end? We all heard that leaked audio, and we watched them deliver the staged and premeditated "deliberate attack, or rather disruption," as they systematically targeted and picked on Ebonyi North Senator Onyekachi Nwebonyi, who had appeared before the Senate Committee on Ethics Privileges and Public Petitions on behalf of Senator Akpabio, which conducted a hearing on the petition brought by Senator Natasha against the Senate President.

The voice in that audio is not just mocking Nigerians; she's mocking the system, the government, and the very institutions of law and order that hold our nation together.

This brings to mind a haunting déjà vu. During the Goodluck Ebele Jonathan administration, what began as allegations of sexual harassment against figures like Reno

Omokri soon escalated into nationwide distractions. The "Bring Back Our Girls" campaign, led again by Dr. Oby Ezekwesili, dominated global headlines and turned domestic vulnerability into an international spectacle.

But the question remains: was it all timed and orchestrated to discredit that government and tip the scales in favor of opposition forces?

Now, nearly a decade later, the same actors are re-emerging with disturbingly similar tactics, weaponized allegations, strategic media campaigns, international lobbying, and highly emotional public manipulation. Is this a coincidence or a conspiracy that should not be ignored?

The leaked audio explicitly references a 2027 political agenda, suggesting that these disruptions are not isolated incidents but part of an allegedly well-funded, well-structured, long-term plan to destabilize the current administration led by President Bola Ahmed Tinubu and reportedly sow discord within the Yoruba political stronghold.

Each time a disruption occurs, be it a media scandal, legal evasion, a labor strike, or regional unrest, we must ask:

- Who benefits from this?

- Who funds the chaos?

- Who controls the narrative behind the scenes?

The tactics of distraction, defamation, and diversion are well-known tools of fifth-column actors and political insurgents.

The repeated targeting of top government officials and allies like Senator Godswill Akpabio and Reno Omokri, coupled with synchronized propaganda across national and international platforms, is not mere activism; it smacks of coordinated subversion.

I firmly believe that the Nigerian government must treat this matter not just as a case of defamation or political agitation but as a potential national security threat. Under both domestic and international law, any individual or group reportedly attempting to manipulate public perception, interfere with judicial processes, or incite unrest for political gain may fall under scrutiny for acts bordering on sedition, criminal conspiracy, and obstruction of justice.

As a concerned citizen and researcher, I have submitted additional findings and recommendations to the appropriate authorities. Therefore, I would like to ask again: who are these people trying to set the country on fire?

- Are these media agents, lawyers, and NGOs acting independently?

- Are they pawns in a wider game of regime change?

- Is the Nigerian public once again being used as collateral damage for 2027 ambitions?

This is not just politics. This looks like a threat to democracy, to law and order, and the sovereignty of the Nigerian state. Hence, the Presidency, security agencies, and the courts must rise to the occasion because these patterns are too dangerous to ignore. We must not allow history to repeat itself under new disguises.

From Chibok to the present courtroom circus, the Benue crisis, the masterminds may be the same. But this time, Nigeria must not fall for the same trick twice. The time to act is now!

"This is not just politics. This is a threat to democracy, to law and order, and to the sovereignty of the Nigerian state. From Chibok to the present courtroom circus, the Benue crisis, the masterminds may be the same. But this time, Nigeria must not fall for the same trick twice." – Prof. Sandra C Duru.

Social Media Reactions | Observations: Valid Facts Or Conspiracy Theories

Another avid reader and follower on social media, named Oreoluwa, raised strong allegations, citing the situation in Benue State, Nigeria. He suggested that Senator Natasha's shenanigans may be linked to a former Vice President and a faction of the PDP.

According to him, *"We've seen this before during GEJ's regime, and it's happening again. Wake up and be wise. Terrorism in Nigeria is actively sponsored for cheap political points."*

Could this be another strategy to deliberately destabilize the current administration and weaken it from within by creating chaos in the country and inciting the people against it? This may sound like a conspiracy theory to many, but to others who care to observe and examine events around them critically, there may be more to this than meets the eye at the moment.

Conclusion: Profit In Chaos: It Is The Art And Way Of Some!

It is no longer a secret that some people gain from crisis and profit from chaos. Hence, they are virtually always positioned to benefit directly or indirectly whenever and wherever there is trouble.

The wise say that if something happens once, it may be a mistake. The second time may be a coincidence, but anything beyond that could be a deliberate pattern that everyone involved would do well to take proper note of and beware of.

"When patterns repeat in calculated cycles, it's no longer mere coincidence; it is strategy. This is not just a call for observation. This is a call for national attention. A dangerous narrative is unfolding beneath the surface, and the signs have become too clear to ignore." – Prof. Sandra C Duru.

CHAPTER 11:

What To Expect When You Stand For Truth: What Should You Do?

"When the law is silent, it is not asleep. It is gathering!" – Prof. Sandra C Duru.

This chapter details all I have been subjected to since I publicly took a stand for the truth and chose not to join forces with Senator Natasha in her vile gender manipulation and malicious gender-based attacks against the innocent.

It is my hope and desire that all who read this will be enlightened through it and also come to know that there is always a price to pay for standing and siding with the truth, especially when it is unpopular. What can you expect when you choose to stand for the truth, and what should you do when these things start happening?

They Will Come For You And All You Hold Dear: Especially Your Name And Honor!

In every case where one party is absolutely bent on

subverting the law and perverting justice, witness intimidation is a core part of the tactics that such despicable elements use. Therefore, be informed now that you will be harassed, attacked, and intimidated, and in no small or kind measure, too!

From my public declaration against the clear gender weaponization agenda of Senator Natasha, it felt like all hell was let loose against me, and every fiber of my life was mindlessly attacked, including my beautiful, innocent children and family members who knew nothing and were not involved with the case in any way.

Such is the intimidation and demoralizing tactic of the chronic manipulator, but you must determine never to be fazed by anything thrown at you. They called me everything from a school dropout to a fugitive. Yet, in their own words, I keep showing up at global high-level meetings, walking freely into Nigeria, the United Kingdom, and the United States of America, having strategic sessions with the likes of Dr Olisa Agbakoba (SAN), top world business executives, and many other respected leaders they could only dream of accessing.

While they were busy climbing ladders of seduction and manipulation to 'achieve' what they call status, I was busy conceptualizing the SONCAP and MANCAP programs as a brilliant consultant, adding value to Nigeria's regulatory framework and shaping policy architecture for generations.

Now, the same pathological liar, Senator Natasha, who once came to me begging to join her and Dr Ezekwesili on their disgraceful campaign of sabotage against Nigeria, President Tinubu's government, and the Senate President, is shaking because she saw my name on the principal witness list against her. So, I'm wondering: *"Why are you shaking if I am everything you have relentlessly claimed and broadcast about me? Why not rest assured because, in your opinion, I am nobody, am I not?"*

Senator Natasha weaponized Adeola Fayehun and her social media podcast, titled *"Keeping It Real With Adeola,"* against me in such a blatantly unprofessional way that even the blind in Nigeria could see that it was all a show of shameless propaganda and desperate mudslinging. From her first public guest against me on May 10, 2025, Francess Ogbonnaya, who eventually turned on her during the pathetic live interview and railed at her to "do her job," to Obinna Akuwudike, her senselessly illiterate supposed expose on me that on further exposed her level of ignorance and desperation to defame me, to David Ronsinski, a deviously lying criminal from America, I strategically, professionally, and publicly debunked all the malicious lies they came to spew against me with jaw-dropping receipts, correspondences, documents, and irrefutable evidences of their false claims and malice.

As all those failed woefully, Adeola developed the effrontery to attack, attempt to ridicule, and baselessly accuse astute men who are the elders and fathers who ensured I received a quality education and upheld values of excellence and integrity. She claimed that they were all publicly endorsing my books and projects because they were all being blackmailed by me. A claim that is not only sorely ridiculous, but also criminally defaming, unsubstantiated, and completely false. My question is: can these noble men who served their country brilliantly and retired with their names untarnished not live normal lives and be able to publicly express their support for me or any other cause they believe in anymore? Standing for the truth has never been a crime. Hence, respect should never be mocked, because simplicity is not shame.

I also destroyed this ludicrous attack with damning receipts, videos, and clear evidence that her move was just another sponsored smear campaign with the desperately pathetic aim of soiling my hard-built reputation. However, I can assure you that I am not letting this slide in the next two decades, so that her eventual outcome and punishment will serve as a cautionary tale for the careless. And if anyone ever dares to attack any of my children again, like they've been doing since the beginning of this saga, and anything happens to them, there will be more than hell to pay for all involved!

Eventually, even their principal, Senator Natasha, had to stoop really low out of sheer desperation and also appeared on the podcast live with Adeola on May 30, 2025, to publicly malign, criminally defame, and brazenly attempt to damage my reputation because I am a principal witness in the ongoing investigation and criminal case against her.

Unfortunately, her efforts were also laughable and fell flat on its face, as many keen observers were quick to publicly ask why she was so bold to show up on the sponsored podcast of lies but refused to turn up for the very important hearing set up to determine the veracity of her sexual harassment claims against the Senate President. Her motives and tactics were also publicly questioned and flawed for appearing on the podcast, seeing that she was the prime suspect in an ongoing criminal investigation and shouldn't even be seen granting media interviews, let alone appearing on a podcast to defame and attempt to intimidate me, a key witness in the case against her.

However, I wasn't shocked or perturbed about her move, and also smartly debunked all her lies with even more damning evidence of her folly and evil schemes right there on social media. I am not a novice in this game, and I had preemptively prepared for all their shenanigans because I have always known that they would vigorously attack my name and reputation.

It's a natural resort for people like her who are steeped in gender weaponization and false allegations, but I made sure always to stay ten steps ahead of them, and I still do to date.

"Give a dog a bad name so you can hang it. If this were so in the days of our fathers, nothing would change it today, and so it will forever be. Those who seek to destroy you will always first seek to tarnish your name, image, and reputation. Protect it fiercely!" – Prof. Sandra C Duru.

They Will Find "Your Judas" And Weaponize Them Against You.

Every great person and leader always has someone or even a group of people within their camp who would not hesitate to sell them out for a loaf of bread. Even the Lord Jesus Christ had a Judas Iscariot among HIS 12 trusted disciples, so rest assured that you may not be immune to this, and they will certainly find and exploit such against you.

In my case, their search for the Judas in my camp did not stop at only one person; they dug deep into my recent and long past and came up with a bunch of laughable,

irrelevant, ludicrously false, and desperately malicious individuals within and without who were well pleased to align with the embattled senator's cause as long as it guaranteed them a fat pay-off and other material benefits.

Their major game was cyberbullying, cyberstalking, criminal defamation with the intent to publicly discredit and destroy my solid image and reputation, intimidation, threats to my life, safety, and well-being, along with my family and close associates, and a barrage of daily harassment all over their compromised social and traditional media outlets, among others.

There were several key players in this plot. Still, the most active ones were Maazi Obinna Akuwudike, Francess Ogbonnaya, Adanna Chinyere, Eze Madumere, Precious Iluo-Oghene, David Ronsinski, and the social media vlogger and influencer named Adeola Fayehun. Of all these, though, my personal Judas here was Obinna Akuwudike.

However, let me make one thing very clear here now:

Obinna is not related to me in any way. He does not know my story, my pain, or the depths of my sacrifice. Yet I treated him, like many others from Imo State, Nigeria, as a brother. With no airs or class distinction, I embraced him with open arms. My humility, my simplicity, and my genuine love were never acts; they are who I am.

He first met me in 2011 when I voluntarily stepped down from the Accord Party gubernatorial ticket for Ken Ojiri and aligned with Owelle Rochas Okorocha, then a board member of my nonprofit, PAAO, and someone I respected as a father. I served Rochas diligently in the areas of security, surveillance, legal matters, and media. Barr. Ope Banwo, IGP (Rtd) Hafiz Ringim, High Chief Bonny Ebili, and H.E. Ikedi Ohakim can all attest to my loyalty. Unfortunately, Rochas, like many others, chose 'hot & cold' betrayal over gratitude, but that's a story for another day.

As for Obinna, he had made betrayal a lifestyle. From H.E. Ikedi Ohakim to Senator Ifeanyi Ararume, Ndaa Jude, and others, he leaves a trail of deceit. I intervened to help Ikedi Ohakim clear his name during his ordeal with an estranged woman because I do not tolerate gender weaponization against men. It is a cause I fight passionately for.

I warned Obinna, helped him, forgave him, prayed for him,

and even preached Christ to him. And each time he stumbled, I quietly rescued him without broadcasting it. Despite the hatred and disrespect, I refuse to respond with the same. I see their evil, but I choose love. That is my strength. That is my identity.

So, I watched with keen interest as some of my political adversaries in Imo State, Nigeria, who facilitated the connection between Obinna and Francess to Emmanuel Uduaghan and his wife, Senator Natasha Akpoti-Uduaghan, attempted to shield their criminal conspiracy to defame my character. It was so blatantly done that it didn't take long to become very evident that financial inducements were exchanged to orchestrate this defamation deliberately.

Obinna received and shared the money with his wife, sister, and others into his over 36 active bank accounts so that he could appear on Adeola's live show of lies on social media. The same was done by Francess, who was also paid to peddle lies and false criminal allegations against me. This is not a game I am unfamiliar with, so I have remained unperturbed by all their shenanigans and fruitless attacks. The rule of law will surely take its course because the clock is ticking, and the truth is not on their side. For everyone else reading this right now, I would like you to know and note this fact below.

When the Law Watches Silently, It's Never Idle. It is Gathering Evidence!

In the realm of federal and international law, especially within the United States of America, cybercrime, stalking, harassment, intimidation, and criminal defamation are not light offenses. They are serious violations that trigger both state and federal investigations, particularly when the victims' safety and mental well-being are repeatedly compromised across state or national borders.

For years, David Ronsinski had persistently engaged in a pattern of cyberstalking, online harassment, bullying, threats, and coordinated intimidation against members of my family and me, even in the face of legally binding restraining orders issued to protect us. Despite relocating to a different state, the torment continued. And as further evidence now shows, he didn't act alone, and monetary benefits were used to incite him against me.

This was another person whom Senator Natasha and Adeola Fayehun also recruited and brought on the latter's live show of shameless falsehood. David tried to replicate the same destructive tactics he previously deployed alongside Ms. Edith Modebe and other prominent Imo State evil leaders during the traumatic period when my unborn son, Dikesinachi, was under severe emotional and spiritual attack in my womb, and I found it both sickening and legally alarming.

Let this be known, though: The authorities are not ignorant, nor are they in haste. What they apparently do not understand is that international and federal law enforcement agencies are empowered to investigate complex, orchestrated crimes, including cyberbullying, defamation, coordinated harassment campaigns, and conspiracies involving multiple actors across jurisdictions. While such investigations may last for days, months, or even years, depending on the nature of the crimes, the strength of the petitions, the high volume of evidence presented, and the threat level posed to the victims, justice will surely be served against any unrepentant offender because there are no statutes of limitations protecting them.

So, I always laugh whenever I see people who defame, conspire to malign, bully, and endanger the life of an innocent and clean person, who somehow believe that they can escape the long arms of the law. A harsh lesson surely awaits them, because the law moves with precision, and it is never asleep.

Hence, I have done my due diligence and meticulously gathered evidence of:

- All their premeditated meetings.

- The audio recordings.

- The videos aired on Adeola Fayehun's YouTube and Facebook platforms maliciously attack me unprovoked.

- Natasha's leaked voice notes, where she reportedly acknowledged Adeola's role, thanked her publicly and privately, hosted some of them in Maitama, Abuja, Nigeria, and even planned to make or even made certain unlawful promises and affidavits to seal their conspiracy.

- Their coordinated smear campaigns.

- Their personal and financial motives.

- Their interactions during Natasha's U.S. visit are all under thorough investigation, particularly in relation to my safety concerns and the documented threats of cybercrime-related attacks I've received.

I am one of the principal witnesses in multiple cases involving these individuals, and what I have not yet released to the public is far greater than what has already been seen. Justice is a process, and I have chosen to proceed strategically, with patience, and in phases.

Hence, let this serve as a reminder to every conspirator and participant:

The law never forgets. The law never forgives deliberate evil easily. And the law never fails when the truth is clear and the evidence undeniable. Justice is coming. Slowly, legally, surely.

"The law forgets nothing. The law fears no conspirator. And I fear no evil because EL-ROI is watching, too. Justice is coming!" – Prof. Sandra C Duru.

You Will Be Up Against Every Machinery: Known And Unknown!

When you choose to stand and fight for the truth in any case, your adversaries, bent on spreading deception and their manipulative agenda, will declare an all-out war and begin to move every existing battle machinery against you.

One of the ways they do this is that they will attempt to control the narrative by putting all the media outlets and bloggers on their payroll and instigating them to attack, bully, and attempt to discredit you publicly. Going up against Senator Natasha and Oby Ezekwesili pit me against their propaganda and smear campaign tools, including Adeola Fayehun, Sowore And His Sahara Reporters, Arise

TV, Rufai Oseni, Reuben Abati, and the likes of them, but I was never fazed or intimidated.

They went as far as publishing false news about a fake allegation against me as part of their relentless smear campaign. Still, the one titled: *"Nigerian Government Lists Woman 'Declared Wanted By Police Since 2016' As Witness To Testify Against Senator Natasha"* by the Sahara Reporters media outlet was the most laughable.

The reported complainant against me failed woefully to substantiate her baseless fraud allegations because there was no evidence whatsoever, no documented business transaction, no receipts, no proof of fraud, and no admissible material to back her claims. And, as we all know, allegations without evidence remain mere noise, and going to the police first does not automatically confer truth or victory.

This case was a domestic matter, and I had overlooked the alleged complainant, Mama Edidot's excesses. To date, she cannot provide any evidence of how I defrauded her or what business we transacted aside from the school fees for my children that I demanded a refund for and got from her.

Education is not just important; it's essential, especially when you're making claims that require legal understanding. Knowing the law saves you from public embarrassment.

So let me make this very clear here now:

•No one is looking for me. I was never and have never been a fugitive! Magistrate court matters are strictly state-level, and they have nothing to do with the federal government, so it is ludicrous even to think or state that I am hiding away in the United States of America as an international fugitive. I have been in and out of Nigeria countless times since this matter was maliciously instituted 10 years ago, so how can I be a fugitive?

•I did not defraud anyone. There was no business transaction or any financial dealing whatsoever between the person who falsely alleged fraud against me to settle a personal grievance. And, to date, no iota of proof has ever been brought forward to substantiate her claim or even initiate a criminal charge against me, so the matter has always been dead on arrival.

•To be candidly clear, Mama Edidot was the proprietress of my children's former school. She gained closer access to my family and me when she begged me to help her with a land dispute she had with someone who had built a petrol station on the border of her land in the Badore, Ajah area of Lagos State, Nigeria, back then. That access eventually led to a domestic challenge between us, and she decided to take advantage of my simplicity and went to the police to allege a false claim against me at the Area J Police Headquarters, Elemoro, in Lekki, Lagos State, Nigeria.

Her statement was taken down, and the police also invited me. After careful cross-examination, the police determined that it was a civil matter and that we should resolve our differences amicably there. Still, she was headstrong and bent on taking a pound of flesh. Hence, she insisted that the matter be brought to court. However, she never came forward to her case hearings because she knew her allegations were trumped up and fabricated, the same way Senator Natasha chose to disrupt the hearing set up to investigate her sexual harassment allegations instead of showing up with concrete evidence to substantiate her claims.

You may also recall that Solomon Arase was appointed Acting IGP on April 21, 2015, and later confirmed. He continued to serve under former President Muhammadu Buhari until June 21, 2016. So, as for IGP Solomon Arase, how could he have been "looking for me" when I was actively and honorably serving Nigeria at that time in my official capacity as a Principal Consultant for the Police Service Commission?

Let's call a spade a spade: Senator Natasha and her cohorts again failed shamefully to discredit and ruin my reputation on this, as they did with everything else they falsely leveled and fabricated against me. Their level of ignorance is loud, embarrassing, and, unfortunately, dangerous, so I am making sure to attend to all legal issues timely and accordingly!

Instead of presenting hard evidence to prove their claims, their entire energy is focused on "exposing" a woman with nothing to hide, from Nigeria to America to the UK. But how do you expose transparency? How do you smear a spotless record? You can't. And that's exactly why they've been rattled.

In the words of Esese Isokun, an avid reader who has followed the whole saga on social media to date: *"God hates a lying tongue. 'The LORD detests lying lips, but he delights in those who tell the truth.' – Proverbs 12:22. Surely, there is an end to everything. Sin has consequences. Let justice prevail."*

The mere mention of my name on the witness list has reportedly turned her and her confused camp into overnight prayer warriors! The fear is real and justified. They've tried everything under the sun (and even beneath it) to destroy my credibility, integrity, and character, galloping from Nigeria to America like confused horses on expired steroids. But what has been the outcome of every single attempt? Epic failure!

Another keen social media observer, Oludotun Oluwole, also raised this valid question and point: *"I'm completely confused! Someone harassed you, and you didn't sue him. He then accused you of defamation and reported the matter to the police for investigation. After the investigation, you're now charged in court, where you can present evidence to support your allegations of sexual harassment that you possess, yet you want the case to be withdrawn from the court. Please, make sense out of this for me."*

Yes, you will be up against every known and unknown tactic and machinery whenever you go to war for the truth, but you must never waver and remain fearless.

***"As long as what you hold is the truth, everything else will fade and become extinct before it eventually, for by it all things were made by the Creator!"** – Prof. Sandra C Duru.*

They Will Make Direct And Indirect Attempts To End Your Life: From Failed Accusations To Assassination Plots!

After a heated conversation I had with Ambrose Nwaogwugwu, one of the aides to the Imo State, Nigeria, Governor Hope Uzodinma, I went online to ask a question and also alert the public after he made brazen threats against my life and safety.

I asked: *"Does this imply that Ambrose, the aide to Governor Hope Uzodinma, is privy to a plot to assassinate me in Nigeria?*

I am gravely concerned about the threats emanating from him, threats which he appears to issue not in his personal capacity but while acting in full representation of his principal, the Executive Governor of Imo State, Hope Uzodinma.

Is it a coincidence that these threats are surfacing amid ongoing obstruction of justice and interference with active criminal investigations linked to the same political circles?

What exactly is Governor Hope Uzodinma trying to shield by preventing due process? Why are those connected to his office repeatedly attempting to intimidate, silence, or endanger me?

Unheard Screams: The Hidden War On (Wo)men

I raise these questions publicly not just for my safety but because the law must never bow to power, and truth must never be assassinated in silence."

Without a shadow of a doubt, please know that one of the things your adversaries will surely target when you go to war for the truth is your life and even those of your family and loved ones if they have such access to you. Hence, you must never take any threats (verbal, written, electronic, physical, direct, implied, anything!) lightly or let them slide. Ensure that they are documented properly, and also raise public alarm about them with substantial evidence.

Since it has become obvious to the world that Natasha has serious cases to answer, she is doing all she can to intimidate and suppress me. Still, alas, no amount of propaganda or manipulation will erase me from the witness list. I see all that I have suffered and had to endure since unveiling her to the world as nothing but a small price to pay for the undiluted truth, genuine peace, and the safety and sanity of the defenseless and voiceless in the world today.

It will take a lot more than just ceaseless cyberbullying, criminal defamation, social and media manipulation, and veiled or direct threats against my life to stop me from seeing this to the end.

Unheard Screams: The Hidden War On (Wo)men

A divine intervention made her path cross with mine for clarity, closure, and justice for the innocent. And, now that she has finally been arraigned and her criminal trial has started, her due retribution for all her gender-based manipulations and sins against the innocent will certainly be meted out to her. This is no longer a tale or a fable. It is a certainty, and the world will witness it sooner rather than later.

After the sinking masterminds of false accusations failed to provide any evidence of their false allegations against me, and their so-called whistleblowers also had nothing to offer, their public show of shame on Adeola Fayehun's YouTube program was quite hilarious, as that has also yielded absolutely nothing. However, after a recent failed attempt to wipe evidence from my device through a compromised police officer investigating Natasha's cases, they have now resorted to using a family member, my village king, his palace secretary, and Eze Madumere to stage yet another coup attempt against me. Unfortunately for them again, though, this plot was dead on arrival, too.

A driver was planted in my ancestral home to bring in "AGBARA" (a local voodoo charm) to kill me, my siblings, and our aged mother. Fortunately, the community leaders apprehended him, and I immediately wrote a petition to the police to investigate this case.

However, while the petition was still active with glaring evidence, documentation, verdicts, minutes, and statements from community leaders, some prominent Imo State politicians hijacked my family's case overnight.

Shockingly, too, the IGP Monitoring Unit Head maliciously took over my straightforward case in an appallingly apparent attempt to fish for gossip. They kept my lawyers and me completely out of our own case, and the Monitoring Unit Head even brazenly denied knowing anything about or being in custody of the case file and the suspect, not knowing that I had already tracked my case file straight to his table. While they've been threatening to eliminate me, I have been busy diligently tracking all their IPs, identifications, and numbers, and I've meticulously kept everything intact until they are needed.

So, no matter what she and her entire gang do to me, I will be here to testify as one of the principal witnesses against her, as already listed by the prosecution. No death, evil, or harm shall ever befall me and all mine before and after I do.

"Only the living can sue for peace, equity, truth, and justice. Do all you can to stay alive and keep safe. The world needs your light and truth!" – **Prof. Sandra C Duru.**

The Battle Rages On Before You: Ignore The Betrayals!

To all my wonderful tribe of truth lovers worldwide, another deep truth I would like you all to note and learn from my encounters with these evil gender weaponization merchants is that you must always learn how to look beyond the Judases in your camp, and all the pain their nasty betrayals bring into your heart.

Do you know why? It's because that betrayal was just a strategic move of the enemy to distract you and make you lose focus on the real purpose and quest before you. Hence, you must wake up and ignore it, because the battle yet rages on before you, and you must never be consumed by it! Stop blaming or focusing on anything or anyone who broke your heart, and look inwards instead, because sometimes, it is your unwillingness to rise above the noise and discomfort of those emotional wounds, plus your lack of wisdom and pettiness, that does the most damage to you, and not the betrayals you're so fixated on.

The enemy plans to keep you in victim mode by making you hold silly grudges, and no one wins a battle that they go into feeling like a victim. You will never recognize your real enemies if you remain this way, and this ensures that you have lost even before the battle begins. Remember the wise words of King Solomon? "A fool gives full vent to his spirit, but a wise man quietly holds it back." - Proverbs 29:11.

I know that these betrayals hurt like crazy, but you must learn to feel and ignore that pain without becoming it. This is true wisdom, and this is how you overcome! Dismiss who you must, crush those who deserve to be, sideline those who are not worthy of your energy quietly, and dismiss those you need to without breaking a sweat or any noise because your eyes are focused only on your ultimate goal. This is how I roll, because it is the way of the truly great, mature, and strategic champions.

My friend and brother, Hon. Uche Nwosu, once testified this about me: *"Whatever Sandra Duru sets her mind to achieve, she will achieve it before she leaves!"* And he's right. I don't get distracted by noise, wailers, attacks, or even applause. I only focus on results, on purpose, and divine timing. I may adjust my strategy, but never the excellence of the outcome, because I am always results-oriented!

Isah Alkali Ibrahim, one of my followers on social media, said, *"Go hard on these gullible and hungry useful idiots!"* and I laughed so hard! However, in the spirit of that moment, I tried to pass a message across to him, and I'll share it with you, too, so you can better understand my point about maintaining focus. I replied:

"My dear brother, Isah, going hard or even harder on someone whose mental libido is on life support and whose stamina can't handle even a tickle of intellectual romance? That's how you cause bedroom mental suicide!

Honestly, it can turn into homicide by overthinking! You'll be arguing with their rotten IQ, and it's ghosting you mid-sentence! Some of them need mental foreplay first, not fire. Because once you fire them with facts, they start convulsing in confusion, speaking in tongues of nonsense."

As fun as that may sound sometimes, to go hard on noisemakers and ignorant minions swarming your page during times like these, please know that it is only a needless distraction that offers nothing but amusement, and that is not what we are here for presently.

The question to you now is, are you also ready to evolve and win, or do you want to continue holding yourself back?

"The only thing you should ever write off is your old self when you finally grow into wisdom, purpose, and power!" – Prof. Sandra C Duru.

What Would Have Happened To Senator Akpabio If There Were No Resolute Truth Crusader Like Sandra Duru?

This question begs an answer right now and also raises disturbing awareness of the now common fact that there are indeed millions of innocent men and women languishing in prisons, police cells, and unlawful detentions worldwide because they were up against adversaries much more influential, powerful, connected, and adept at gender weaponization and manipulation than they were.

It also raises a valid yet disturbing food for thought: If this could have happened to a person as hugely influential and connected as the Senate President of the Federal Republic of Nigeria, Senator Godswill Akpabio, what is now the fate of the common and average woman, man, girl, and boy out there who have no power, money, connections, influence, or the voice to cry out for help against their strong adversaries and be heard?

Like Prince Abdulkareem Onyekehi commented after I effortlessly and confidently rebuffed another of the incessant waves of cyberbullying and reputation-destroying attacks against me online, *"God positioned me for the wrong call from the wrong person who stepped on the wrong toes for the wrong reasons as an opportunity for the divine intervention on your unprecedented, untiring passion and energy against agents of destructions from their manipulation, fabrication of falsehoods, false accusations and gender weaponization."* For this, I say, as always, let God alone be praised!

However, do you have any idea how many innocent men are languishing in police detention, prison, without any trial or fair hearing over unsubstantiated accusations like Senator Natasha's tirade against Senator Akpabio? Do you also know how many (wo)men are dying slowly with unheard screams in their marriages because their supposed spouses are gender weaponization specialists?

The truth about these statistics will break your heart terribly, but it will also open your eyes to the need for all of us to band together and take a firm stand against this demonic tool being used to destroy so many innocent lives. Again, I ask, if God had not somehow pushed her to me and also made her inexplicably spill her guts the way she did, wouldn't Senator Akpabio have been facing impeachment, career, social, and family destruction, and also become a national and international disgrace by now? All because one woman felt aggrieved and decided to play the gender weaponization card against him.

My experiences and encounters in the course of this saga compel me to beg everyone reading this right now:

Please, don't ever judge or condemn anyone until you have objectively heard and thoroughly examined the case or charges against them. Never succumb to crocodile tears or cheap emotional manipulation of anyone playing the gender card; such evil people are usually very adept at such things, and they can easily fool anyone not sensitive or grounded enough.

The more our societies decide never to condemn anyone until they're irrefutably proven guilty with accurate, genuine, and compelling evidence, the less we would have to face and deal with this scourge of gender weaponization, which continuously births unheard screams for help in so many helpless and defenseless lives.

This fight is real, and we must all partake to save all our (wo)men, girls, and boys because, if this could happen to someone as seemingly powerful and affluent as Senator Akpabio, what chances of survival do they have if we don't?

"This is no longer a personal fight. This is a divine battle for the soul of truth, justice, and national integrity. And we're not backing down." – Prof. Sandra C Duru.

The Urgency Of Truth: Why Senator Natasha's Baseless Sexual Harassment Claim Against Senator Akpabio Cannot Just Be Swept Under The Carpet

As the Nigerian nation and the world continued to await the irrefutable and conclusive evidence of Senator Natasha Akpoti-Uduaghan's sexual harassment claims against Senator Godswill Akpabio, the Senate President took the much-needed and wise legal decision to file a Two Hundred Billion Naira (N200b) defamation lawsuit against the Kogi Central Senator.

In his suit, he accused her of publishing malicious and unfounded allegations that he sexually harassed her, and he demanded extensive damages, formal retractions, and nationwide broadcast apologies because her claims had gained massive online circulation despite lacking substantiation. Senator Akpabio also insisted that Natasha's allegations gravely injured his reputation and subjected him to widespread public ridicule.

Unheard Screams: The Hidden War On (Wo)men

HOLDEN AT...
BEFORE HIS LORDSHIP:
HON. JUSTICE U. P. KEKEMEKE, ACIArb (UK), FICMC
THIS 6TH DAY OF NOVEMBER, 2025

SUIT NO. FCT/HC/CV/3356/2025
MOTION NO. M/12725/2025

BETWEEN:
SENATOR GODSWILL OBOT AKPABIO, GCON .... CLAIMANT/APPLICANT
AND
SENATOR NATASHA AKPOTI-UDUAGHAN .... DEFENDANT

COURT ORDER

UPON READING THE MOTION PAPER DATED 10/10/2025 BROUGHT EXPARTE AND THE AFFIDAVIT in Support, praying this Honourable Court for the following reliefs:

1. AN ORDER of the Honourable Court granting leave to the Claimant/Applicant to serve the Originating Processes, i.e. Writ of Summons and all other subsequent processes including Hearing Notices in this Suit, (Suit No. FCT/HC/CV/3356/2025) on the Defendant by substituted means to wit, by delivering same to the Clerk of the National Assembly, or any staff in the office of the Clerk of the National Assembly, Three Arms Zone, Abuja, Federal Capital Territory.

2. AN ORDER of the Honourable Court deeming the said mode of service of the processes on the Defendant as good and proper service.

3. AND for such further or other Order(s) as the Honourable Court may deem fit to make in the circumstances of this case.

Image 22: Senate President, Godswill Akpabio, files ₦200 Billion defamation lawsuit against Senator Natasha Akpoti-Uduaghan.

Unheard Screams: The Hidden War On (Wo)men

The case titled FCT HC CV 3356 2025 and accompanied by Motion No M 12725 2025 revolves around Akpabio's assertion that the allegations inflicted deep personal and professional harm. Through an ex parte application filed in December 2025, he sought permission to serve court processes on Senator Natasha via substituted means.

Presiding over the matter at the High Court of the Federal Capital Territory, Abuja, Nigeria, Justice Kekemeke granted the request and ruled that all originating and subsequent documents should be delivered to the Clerk of the National Assembly or any staff in the Clerk's office at the Three Arms Zone in Abuja. The Honourable Court also deemed this method of service as valid and proper in the circumstances, thus clearing the path for the suit to proceed after earlier attempts to serve Senator Natasha directly had proved abortive.

Senator Akpabio's Statement of Claim, backed by listed witnesses, underscored how interviews granted by Senator Akpoti on radio, television, and digital platforms portrayed him as a predator who used his office for personal gratification. He argued that millions of Nigerians consumed these broadcasts, generating a wave of backlash that he described as humiliating, distressing, and deeply damaging.

Hence, he urged the court to compel the removal of all online content containing the allegations and to mandate an apology repeatedly aired across major media outlets for several consecutive days. A court order issued on November 6, 2025, officially authorized this substituted service, allowing the claimant to move forward with the matter. Both parties now prepare for what is projected to be one of the most closely watched political and legal battles in Nigeria.

The Senate President not only survived a storm, but the gravity of what he faced must not be ignored. He survived a dangerous attempt at gender weaponization, media manipulation, and character assassination. Nigeria owes itself the truth. Hence, closure is essential, not only for the man at the center of these allegations but for the integrity of every institution that stands to be weakened when falsehood is allowed to flourish unchecked.

Justice must prevail, and the truth must stand tall!

"In every nation that values justice, truth, and accountability, closure is not a luxury. It is a necessity. This moment calls for courage. It calls for truth. And above all, it calls for closure!" – Prof. Sandra C Duru.

Conclusion: This Is A Fight For All!

Let me make something crystal clear to every misinformed, willfully ignorant, and hypocritically silent person or group of persons on this matter: I owe no respect to characters born by wickedness, fraud, sustained by deceit, and fueled by cowardice!

And if you still think that I am doing too much, or more than the person directly affected, let me tell you this today: I am not speaking for Nigeria, not representing the Senate, and I'm certainly not speaking for any politician. I am defending myself, my name, my children, and my legacy, and I am standing unshakably on the side of truth and justice.

If Senator Natasha Akpoti-Uduaghan had not walked into my life carrying the stinking load of her lies, false allegations, and vile tales of corruption and deception against Senator Godswill Akpabio and even her own country, Nigeria, I would never have gotten involved. But she did. And because she did, I have taken it upon myself to dismantle, brick by brick, the empire of manipulation and slander she tried to build on sand.

What she never realized, but is now finding out in the toughest way, is that I am a deeply spiritual, intuitive, intelligent, and highly sensitive person who never jokes with her altar of fire, meditations, and ceaseless prayers for God's guidance and help always. Hence, I can almost affirm that coming to me and opening up about the alleged sexual harassment and all those other devious accusations she's been trying to hide behind was no accident but a divinely orchestrated event.

After cunningly manipulating and enrolling the likes of Dr Ezekwesili, Dr Abiola, and Rufai Oseni of Arise TV to push her agenda and run her dirty errands, she felt I could also be lured into her manipulative schemes against Senator Akpabio and President Tinubu as part of their alleged grand plot to destroy the political roadmap to 2027. However, she got that terribly wrong, and now, the world has heard the leaked tapes, and the evidence is no longer hidden.

Do you know that she has stopped at nothing to destroy me since I uncovered her plots and made them public? Her hypocrisy has seen her recruit and pay people like Maazi Obinna Akuwudike, Francess Ogbonna, Adeola Fayehun, and others to defame and make vile and unfounded allegations against me relentlessly. They have posted, said, and done all sorts of tireless cyberbullying and criminal defamation against me before the whole world, all without a shred of evidence, and you still ask why I speak up. They have all the blogs, bloggers, journalists, television, and newspapers, and all I have is God, undiluted truth, and my small social media platforms. Yet the truth is traveling around undisputed and crystal clear! Truth is inestimable and golden!

I was not raised to be a coward. I did not crawl out of a nameless background. I was born and bred in Mbano. And let me tell you, we don't take nonsense there. My foster parents in Southwestern Nigeria, the United States, and India did not raise a mute lamb for slaughter. I was raised to stand, speak, and strike when necessary.

So let me make myself as clear as possible right now: I am fighting back in my way, on my terms, and to the fullest extent that I deem necessary. And, please, no one should ever credit this battle to "sponsorship" or anything political because nobody is funding me. My fantastic petitions against Senator Natasha and her cohorts were all drafted independently by me, and my legal teams, the majority of whom were Senior Advocates of Nigeria (SANs), were all assembled with my resources.

No one should make a mockery of this fight by labeling it "sponsored" because I am facing my persecutors, old and new, including my recycled political enemies from Imo State, Nigeria, with the same fire that brought them to their knees in the past. And this time, they will not rise again.

Unheard Screams: The Hidden War On (Wo)men

Have you ever wondered why some high-ranking government officials suddenly unleashed their media arsenal against me the moment I dismantled Senator Natasha's facade? Why was it Eze Madumere who reportedly connected Obinna and Francess to Senator Natasha Akpoti-Uduaghan and Emmanuel Uduaghan? Why did they pay them to appear on Adeola Fayehun's propaganda machine to spew lies against me?

It's because I am one of the principal witnesses in the ongoing criminal trials against Natasha. That's why, and because the truth terrifies them. They even stooped so low and went as far as having a lowly governor's aide publish an open letter attempting to deride me by calling the Senate President to order because I refused to play ball and be part of their dirty, bitter politics and stand resolutely by an innocent man being vilified unjustly.

If you knew my history, you would know that I do not tolerate disrespect. I do not play in the mud unless I intend to drown my opponent in it. I respect my elders, yes, but only those who respect themselves. If you mess with me, I will mess with you brutally and smartly, too.

If only Senator Natasha had listened to my wise counsel, none of this disgrace would have happened. But no, she chose arrogance over wisdom and thought herself too big to be advised.

I blame her husband and the so-called elder, Dr. Oby Ezekwesili, for failing to stop her. I even suggested a peaceful dialogue, a roundtable, and even a closed-door peace talk in any location of her choice, all facilitated and sponsored by me, but she refused.

Natasha, I've been seated at the highest and most tables of influence long before you even dreamed of stepping near the corridors of power, so don't test me. You cannot conquer the truth because the truth is the very air I breathe, the language I speak, and the cause I live and would die for.

So, if you know that you cannot handle the truth, kindly remove yourself from the stage of relevance because this isn't a play for cowards or clowns. I stand undaunted. I stand unapologetic. I stand unchained. And the truth stands with me. This is why nobody can ever intimidate me, because I stand for the truth until my last breath!

"I was not raised to be a coward. I did not crawl out of a nameless background. I was raised to stand, speak, and strike when necessary, so I can never be intimidated!" – *Prof. Sandra C Duru.*

Unheard Screams: The Hidden War On (Wo)men

The final chapter will be a call to action, urging every (wo)man who reads this book to join the movement and change the world.

The fight continues.

CHAPTER 12:

A Call To Action: Rise, Resist, Reclaim

"The war against (wo)men is silent, but our response must be deafening. Rise, resist, and reclaim your power!"
– Prof. Sandra C. Duru.

We have exposed the hidden war against (wo)men: the harassment, the discrimination, the bullying, and the intimidation that too many men and women endure in silence. Now, it is time to act.

This chapter is a rallying cry for every woman, man, girl, and boy who refuses to be a victim. It is time to rise, resist, and reclaim what belongs to us: our rights, our dignity, and our future.

Rise: Recognizing Your Power

The first step in change is recognizing the power within you. You are not weak, you are not powerless, and you are not alone.

How to Rise Above Oppression:

 1. Educate Yourself: Knowledge is a weapon. Learn your legal rights, study harassment policies, and know the laws that protect you.

2. Build Inner Strength: Work on your confidence, self-worth, and mental resilience.
3. Surround Yourself with Supportive People: Find mentors, allies, and friends who uplift and protect you.
4. Reject Fear and Shame: Do not let society silence you with guilt or intimidation.

"The moment you realize your worth, the battle begins to shift in your favor." – Prof. Sandra C. Duru.

Resist: Fighting Back Against Harassment And Injustice

The systems that enable harassment thrive on silence and submission. To resist means refusing to be silent and refusing to back down.

Ways to Actively Resist Oppression:

- Report Every Incident: No matter how small, speak up! File reports, gather evidence, and expose abusers.
- Confront Harassers Directly: If safe to do so, challenge inappropriate behavior immediately.
- Demand Policy Changes: Advocate for stronger anti-harassment laws and workplace protections.
- Boycott and Protest: Refuse to support businesses, leaders, and institutions that protect abusers.
- Use Social Media as a Weapon: Expose corruption, share stories, and amplify (wo)men's voices.

"Resistance is not just about fighting back; it's about refusing to let oppression win." – Prof. Sandra C. Duru.

Reclaim: Owning Your Space and Future

(Wo)men have been pushed aside for too long. It is time to reclaim what has been stolen: our voices, our leadership, our dignity, and our future.

How to Take Back Your Power:

• Enter Leadership Positions: If the system doesn't protect us, we must take over the system.
• Support Other (Wo)men: Lift men and women who are fighting the same battle.
• Create Safe Spaces for Girls and Boys: Schools, workplaces, and homes must become places of empowerment.
• Teach the Next Generation: Educate young girls and boys on their rights so they grow up fearless.
• Control the Narrative: Write, speak, and document our truths so history cannot erase us.

Another vital thing you must do is never to accept the **"Predator's Doctrine."** The first thing a sexual predator always seeks to do is to publicly discredit you whenever you summon the courage to come forward and expose their vile nature.

If you boldly call their bluff and refuse to back down, they may choose to switch to the nauseatingly evil doctrine of claiming that it is even an honor for you to have them touch your body or make inappropriate passes at you. You are too priceless and dignified ever to take such degrading bait, so you must resist such doctrines, ideologies, concepts, insinuations, suggestions, thoughts, and words as vehemently as you would a thief trying to rob you of your precious jewels!

"We are not guests in this world; we belong here, and we will take our place." – Prof. Sandra C. Duru.

Join The Movement: Be a Part of the Change

The fight is not over, and we need every woman and ally to stand together. Here's how you can join the movement and make a difference:

Ways to Get Involved:

- Start a Conversation: Talk about these issues in your community, workplace, and home.
- Support (Wo) men-led Organizations: Donate, volunteer, or amplify their work.
- Educate Young Girls and Boys: Teach them early so they grow up strong.
- Engage with Lawmakers: Demand policy changes and legal reforms.

- Never Stay Silent: Every voice counts. Every action matters.

"A movement starts with one person. Be that person." – Prof. Sandra C. Duru.

To Every Seemingly Disadvantaged Person Reading This:

This war has been waged against us for generations, but we are the generation that fights back.

We are the (wo)men who refuse to be silenced.
We are the warriors who will never bow to intimidation.
We are the leaders who will create a world where our daughters and sons will never have to scream unheard.

"They tried to silence us. They failed. Now, we rise." – Prof. Sandra C. Duru.

Final Words: The Power of Definition and the Wisdom of Timing

My late father imparted a lesson that has remained etched in my memory: "The extent to which your life is rewarded depends on the quality of the knowledge you possess." This profound insight speaks to a fundamental truth: many individuals falter not because life is inherently unfair, but because their definitions of success, purpose, and reality are fundamentally flawed.

Our greatest undoing often stems from an inability to truly understand others and a failure to articulate our own definitions clearly. To remain true to oneself and achieve genuine fulfillment, one must learn to discern who deserves a place in one's life and who should be cast aside like excess baggage.

He would often remind me, "One of the greatest powers bestowed upon you is the ability to define your reality and your reason for existence. This is your purpose, and within it lies your strength." He always asked me to consider this: "If you are sixty years old and possess the knowledge typical of your peers, you are merely intelligent. However, if you are thirty-five or forty-five and already understand what most sixty-year-olds know, you transcend mere intelligence; you embody wisdom and exceptional gift."

"Wisdom is seeing what is obvious while it is still a secret," he would always say, while also frequently urging me, "I do not wish for you to become a billionaire at ninety-seven. I want you to build your homes, own your estates, and drive your luxury cars. Attain greater success while you still have the life and time to enjoy it."

The years it takes many to achieve their goals often reflect limited knowledge rather than an inherent delay in the process. If one possesses the right understanding, progress can be swift, regardless of the obstacles that lie ahead.

Unheard Screams: The Hidden War On (Wo)men

No external force can derail you if you are equipped with the right knowledge.

He would pause, his voice steady with conviction, and say, "Anything you cannot define will eventually overwhelm you. But what you can define, you can modify." He emphasized the importance of being in total control of your life, decisions, and time, rather than being controlled by organized groups or external powers.

Finally, he imparted a truth that continues to resonate within me: "Do not be money-conscious or materialistic. Be firm, principled, and fearless enough to confront anyone, regardless of their wealth, age, position, or power, when they choose the path of evil. Fear no man, only God. Those you fear today may not see tomorrow, but God can shape you into whoever He desires, with or without the approval of mere mortals."

These words from my beloved father, Pa. B. C. Duru, have been a guiding light on my journey, shaping my destiny in profound ways.

Define your life. Define your purpose. Define your reality. Above all, define your truth before the world attempts to impose its definitions upon you.

In this spirit, I introduce TruthShield, a timely initiative and a global defense against false accusations, media manipulation, and the weaponization of gender. This movement is not political; it is historical.

Unheard Screams: The Hidden War On (Wo)men

It represents a global awakening, conceptualized by me, a universal citizen, and aimed at protecting and defending the rights of men, boys, and families worldwide. Born from the principles of truth, justice, and compassion, TruthShield seeks to ensure that the unheard cries of our men and boys are finally acknowledged, respected, and acted upon.

Project TruthShield will be unveiled in the United States in November 2025, and I want to say a big congratulations to all the men and boys around the world!

My father's wisdom continues to guide me each day. He once said, "Wisdom is seeing what is obvious while it is still a secret." These words remind me that clarity and definition shape our destinies. They inspire me to live with courage and conviction, fearing no one but God. I place my faith in His power to shape my life, not in the approval of any human being whose next breath is uncertain. That is my TruthShield.

So, let's rise together. Let's resist oppression. Let's reclaim our power!

"Unheard Screams: The Hidden War On (Wo)men" is not just a book: It is a call to arms.

Are you ready to fight?

APPENDICES

Appendix A: Key Legal Frameworks Protecting Women Against Harassment and Discrimination

1. International Laws and Conventions

Several global legal frameworks protect women's rights. Understanding these laws can help women recognize and assert their rights. These laws include, and are not limited to, the following:

• The United Nations Convention on the Elimination of All Forms of Discrimination Against Women (CEDAW): A global treaty adopted in 1979 to eliminate discrimination against women.
• The Universal Declaration of Human Rights (UDHR): Recognizes gender equality as a fundamental human right.
• The International Labour Organization (ILO) Convention No. 190: The first international law to specifically address workplace violence and harassment.
• The African Charter on Human and Peoples' Rights (Maputo Protocol): A legal framework specific to Africa that promotes women's rights and protects against gender-based violence.

2. National Laws Protecting Women in Africa

Different African countries have laws against gender-based violence, harassment, and discrimination.

Here are some examples:

- Nigeria: The Violence Against Persons Prohibition Act (VAPP) criminalizes sexual harassment and domestic violence.
- South Africa: The Sexual Offences Act strengthens legal action against sexual harassment and rape.
- Kenya: The Sexual Offences Act criminalizes sexual exploitation and harassment in workplaces and institutions.
- Ghana: The Domestic Violence Act protects women from abuse in homes and workplaces.
- Namibia:

Women must educate themselves on their country's legal framework and use these laws to demand justice.

Appendix B: Reporting and Support Resources for Women and Girls

1. Where to Report Sexual Harassment and Discrimination

If you are experiencing harassment, discrimination, or bullying, there are official channels you can use:

• Workplace: Report to HR, union representatives, or a legal officer.
• Educational Institutions: Report to school authorities, student affairs offices, or gender-based violence desks.
• Police and Legal Institutions: If the harassment is criminal, file a police report.
• NGOs and Women's Rights Organizations: Many organizations offer legal assistance, counseling, and safe spaces for women.

2. Global and African Organizations Supporting Women

These organizations provide legal help, psychological support, and advocacy for women facing harassment and discrimination:
• UN Women (Global): A UN entity advocating for gender equality.
• Women at Risk International Foundation (Nigeria): Supports survivors of abuse.

- Gender-Based Violence Command Centre (South Africa): Provides emergency assistance for victims.
- Equality Now (Africa & Global): Focuses on legal advocacy for women's rights.
- Federation of Women Lawyers (FIDA): Offers free legal services for women.

Appendix C: Sample Harassment Complaint Letter

If you ever need to file a formal complaint about harassment or discrimination, below is a sample template:

[Your Name]
[Your Address]
[Your Contact Information]
[Date]

To: [HR Manager/Supervisor/Authority Figure]
[Company/Institution Name]
[Company/Institution Address]

Subject: Formal Complaint of Sexual Harassment

Dear [Recipient's Name],

I am writing to formally report an incident of sexual harassment that occurred on [date] at [location]. The individual involved is [Name of Harasser], who holds the position of [Title] in [Department].

The incident(s) involved [describe in detail what happened, including dates, times, and any witnesses]. This behavior has made me feel [explain how it has affected you: unsafe, uncomfortable, discriminated against, etc.].

I request that an immediate investigation be conducted

into this matter, and I seek appropriate action in line with [Company/Institution]'s policies and relevant legal frameworks. I would appreciate a written response outlining the steps that will be taken.

Please consider this complaint confidential, and I expect protection from retaliation. I look forward to your response within [mention a reasonable time frame].

Sincerely,
[Your Name]

Appendix D: 50 Inspirational Quotes by Prof. Sandra C. Duru

1. "When a corrupt system sees a fearless woman rising, they panic. When that woman knows her rights, they tremble. And when she stands firm, they fall!"

2. "Women's voices are weapons. That's why oppressive systems work so hard to silence them."

3. "A strong woman stands alone. An unstoppable woman builds an army."

4. "The moment you realize your worth, the battle begins to shift in your favor."

5. "Resistance is not just about fighting back; it's about refusing to let oppression win."

6. "If the system won't give us justice, we will force it to."

7. "A woman in power is not just a leader. She is a revolution."

8. "They tried to silence us. They failed. Now, we rise."

Unheard Screams: The Hidden War On (Wo)men

9. "We are not guests in this world. We belong here, and we will take our place."

10. "The best revenge against oppression is not survival; it is legacy."

11. "Women are not weak. We have simply been told for too long that we are."

12. "Courage is not the absence of fear; it is the refusal to let fear win."

13. "A single voice may seem small, but when joined with others, it becomes an unbreakable force."

14. "Every injustice exposed is a step toward a just world."

15. "Fear is the tool of the oppressor. Courage is the weapon of the warrior."

16. "We will no longer whisper our pain; we will scream until the world hears."

17. "Empower a woman, and you empower a generation."

18. "There is no such thing as a voiceless (wo)man; only those the world refuses to listen to."

Unheard Screams: The Hidden War On (Wo)men

19. "They called us weak. Now they fear our strength."

20. "(Wo)men's rights are human rights. No debate."

21. "When a woman stands, she stands for millions."

22. "They tell us to wait for justice. We tell them justice delayed is injustice served."

23. "We will not bow. We will not break. We will rise."

24. "The world fears an educated, fearless, and united woman."

25. "Your voice is your power. Use it."

26. "Oppression is loud, but our resistance must be louder."

27. "Never shrink yourself to fit into a broken system. Break the system instead."

28. "The burden of change should not be on women, but we will carry it if we must."

29. "A woman's worth is not defined by the limits men place on her."

30. "We are rewriting history; not as victims, but as warriors."

31. "Power is not given to women. It is taken, demanded, and seized."

32. "When we support each other, nothing can stop us."

33. "The time for apologies is over. The time for action is now."

34. "A woman who refuses to be silent is the most dangerous force in the world."

35. "Men who fear strong women should fear their downfall instead."

36. "You were not born to obey. You were born to lead."

37. "Silence is a weapon they use against us. We must disarm them with our voices."

38. "A world that respects women is a world that thrives."

39. **"Your mind is your greatest asset; you have to boldly and fearlessly sharpen it with confidence, courage,**

intelligence, mental agility, and unshakable toughness. These qualities will shape your success. But above all, put God first in everything you do, oh yes! He is the foundation on which true greatness is built."

40. "Justice is not a gift. It is a right we must claim."

41. "Women do not need permission to be powerful."

42. "Dignity is non-negotiable. Speak. Even if your voice shakes!"

43. "No more whispers. No more waiting. No more injustice."

44. "Every woman's victory is a victory for all of us."

45. "The era of silence is over. We are here, we are loud, and we are unstoppable."

46. "Petty people demand from others what they can't even offer themselves. They nurse their wounds, carry grudges, and write off everyone who betrays them and everyone who isn't perfect, until they eventually write off themselves too."

47. "A fearless (wo)man is a revolution. Rise, resist, reclaim!"

48. "This is our time to lead. Together, we are invincible."

49. "Do yourself a favor and read a textbook, not headlines. This is not the era of mob justice or roadside 'petty' legal theatrics. Some of us were trained to think, speak, and act within the law, not just shout it."

50. "Justice is coming, and we are bringing it."

THE END.

www.ingramcontent.com/pod-product-compliance
Lightning Source LLC
Chambersburg PA
CBHW050516100526
4458ICB00001B/1